PYTHON
MACHINE LEARNING
FOR BEGINNERS

LEARNING FROM SCRATCH NUMPY, PANDAS,
MATPLOTLIB, SEABORN, SCIKITLEARN,
AND TENSORFLOW FOR MACHINE LEARNING
AND DATA SCIENCE

Contains Exercises with solutions and Hands-on Projects

AI PUBLISHING

How to Contact Us

If you have any feedback, please let us know
by sending an email to contact@aispublishing.net.

Your feedback is immensely valued,
and we look forward to hearing from you.
It will be beneficial for us
to improve the quality of our books.

To get the Python codes and materials used in this book,
please click the link below:

https://www.aispublishing.net/book-pmlds

The order number is required.

About the Publisher

At AI Publishing Company, we have established an international learning platform specifically for young students, beginners, small enterprises, startups, and managers who are new to data science and artificial intelligence.

Through our interactive, coherent, and practical books and courses, we help beginners learn skills that are crucial to developing AI and data science projects.

Our courses and books range from basic introduction courses to language programming and data science to advanced courses for machine learning, deep learning, computer vision, big data, and much more. The programming languages used include Python, R, and some data science and AI software.

AI Publishing's core focus is to enable our learners to create and try proactive solutions for digital problems by leveraging the power of AI and data science to the maximum extent.

Moreover, we offer specialized assistance in the form of our online content and eBooks, providing up-to-date and useful insight into AI practices and data science subjects, along with eliminating the doubts and misconceptions about AI and programming.

Our experts have cautiously developed our contents and kept them concise, short, and comprehensive so that you can understand everything clearly and effectively and start practicing the applications right away.

We also offer consultancy and corporate training in AI and data science for enterprises so that their staff can navigate through the workflow efficiently.

With AI Publishing, you can always stay closer to the innovative world of AI and data science.

If you are eager to learn the A to Z of AI and data science but have no clue where to start, AI Publishing is the finest place to go.

Please contact us by email at contact@aispublishing.net.

AI Publishing is Looking for Authors Like You

Interested in becoming an author for AI Publishing? Please contact us at author@aispublishing.net.

We are working with developers and AI tech professionals just like you to help them share their insights with the global AI and Data Science lovers. You can share all your knowledge about hot topics in AI and Data Science.

Table of Contents

Preface

Thank you for your decision on purchasing this book. I can assure you that you will not regret your decision. The saying data is the new oil is no longer a mere cliché. Data is actually powering the industries of today. Organizations and companies need to improve their growth, which depends on correct decision making. Accurate decision making requires facts and figures and statistical analysis of data. Data science does exactly that. With data and machine learning, you can extract and visualize data in detail and create statistical models, which, in turn, help you in decision making. In this book, you will learn all these concepts. So, buckle up for a journey that may give you your career break!

§ Book Approach

The book follows a very simple approach. It is divided into 10 chapters. The first five chapters of the book are dedicated to data analysis and visualization, while the last five chapters are based on machine learning and statistical models for data science. Chapter 1 provides a very brief introduction to data science and machine learning and provides a roadmap for step by step learning approach to data science and machine learning. The process for environment setup, including the software needed to run scripts in this book, is also explained in this chapter.

Chapter 2 contains a crash course on Python for beginners. If you are already familiar with Python, you can skip Chapter 2. Chapter 3 and chapter 4 explain the use of NumPy and Pandas libraries, respectively, for data analysis. Chapter 5 explains the process of data visualization using Python's data visualization libraries such as Matplotlib, Seaborn, and Pandas.

Chapters 6 and 7 provide an introduction to supervised machine learning approaches like regression and classification with the help of the Scikit Learn library. Chapter 8 explains unsupervised machine learning, where you study different clustering approaches for machine learning. Chapter 9 details the introduction to deep learning with TensorFlow 2.0 library, where you will study densely connected neural networks, recurrent neural networks, and convolutional neural networks. Finally, dimensionality reduction approaches have been discussed in the 10th chapter of this book.

In each chapter, an explanation of theoretical concepts is followed by practical examples. Each chapter also contains exercises that students can use to evaluate their understanding of the concepts explained in the chapter. The Python notebook for each chapter is provided in the *Source Codes* folder in the GitHub repository. It is advised that instead of copying the code, you write the code yourself, and in case of an error, you match your code with the corresponding Python notebook, find and then correct the error. You can download the datasets used in this book either at runtime or in the *Datasets* folder in the GitHub repository.

§ Who Is This Book For?

This book explains different data science and machine learning concepts with the help of examples using various Python libraries. The book is aimed ideally at absolute beginners to data science and machine learning. Though a background in the Python programming language and feature engineering can help speed up learning, the book contains a crash course on Python programming language in the first chapter. Therefore, the only prerequisites to efficiently using this book are access to a computer with internet and basic knowledge of linear algebra and calculus. All the codes and datasets have been provided. However, to download data preparation libraries, you will need the internet.

§ How to Use This Book?

As I said earlier, data science and machine learning concepts taught in this book have been divided into multiple chapters. To get the best out of this book, I would suggest that you first get your feet wet with the Python programming language, especially the object-oriented programming concepts. To do so, you can take the crash course on Python in chapter 2 of this book. Also, try to read the chapters of this book in order since the concepts taught in subsequent chapters are based on the concepts in previous chapters.

In each chapter, try to first understand the theoretical concepts behind different types of data science and machine learning techniques and then try to execute the example code. I would again stress that rather than copying and pasting code, try to write codes yourself, and in case of any error, you can match your code with the source code provided in the book as well as in the Python notebooks in the *Source Codes* folder in the

GitHub repository. Finally, try to answer the questions asked in the exercises at the end of each chapter. The solutions to the exercises have been given at the end of the book.

About the Author

M. Usman Malik holds a Ph.D. in Computer Science from Normandy University, France, with Artificial Intelligence and Machine Learning being his main areas of research. Muhammad Usman Malik has over five years of industry experience in Data Science and has worked with both private and public sector organizations. In his free time, he likes to listen to music and play snooker.

Get in Touch With Us

Feedback from our readers is always welcome.

For general feedback, please send us an email at contact@aispublishing.net and mention the book title in the subject line.

Although we have taken extraordinary care to ensure the accuracy of our content, errors do occur. If you have found an error in this book, we would be grateful if you could report this to us as soon as you can.

If you are interested in becoming an AI Publishing author and if you have expertise in a topic and you are interested in either writing or contributing to a book, please send us an email at author@aispublishing.net.

An Important Note to Our Valued Readers:
Download the Color Images

Our print edition books are available only in black & white at present. However, the digital edition of our books is available in color PDF.

We request you to download the PDF file containing the color images of the screenshots/diagrams used in this book here:

https://www.aispublishing.net/book-pmld

The typesetting and publishing costs for a color edition are prohibitive. These costs would push the final price of each book to $50, which would make the book less accessible for most beginners.

We are a small company, and we are negotiating with major publishers for a reduction in the publishing price. We are hopeful of a positive outcome sometime soon. In the meantime, we request you to help us with your wholehearted support, feedback, and review.

For the present, we have decided to print all of our books in black & white and provide access to the color version in PDF. This is a decision that would benefit the majority of our readers, as most of them are students. This would also allow beginners to afford our books.

1

Introduction and Environment Set Up

Data science libraries exist in various programming languages. However, you will be using Python programming language for data science and machine learning since Python is flexible, easy to learn, and offers the most advanced data science and machine learning libraries. Furthermore, Python has a huge data science community where you can take help from whenever you want.

In this chapter, you will see how to set up the Python environment needed to run various data science and machine learning libraries. The chapter also contains a crash Python course for absolute beginners in Python. Finally, the different data science and machine learning libraries that we are going to study in this book have been discussed. The chapter ends with a simple exercise.

1.1. Difference between Data Science and Machine Learning

Data science and machine learning are terms that are often interchangeably used. However, the two terms are different. Data science is a subject area of that uses scientific approaches and mathematical techniques such as statistics to draw out meaning and insights from data. According to Dr. Thomas Miller from Northwestern University, data science is "a combination of information technology, modeling and business management."

Machine learning, on the other hand, is an approach that consists of mathematical algorithms that enable computers to make decisions without being explicitly performed. Rather, machine learning algorithms learn from data, and then based on the insights from the dataset, make decisions without human input.

In this book, you will learn both Data Science and Machine Learning. In the first five chapters, you will study the concepts required to store, analyze, and visualize the datasets. From the 6th chapter onwards, different types of machine learning concepts are explained.

1.2. Steps in Learning Data Science and Machine Learning

1. Know What Data Science and Machine Learning Is All About

Before you delve deep into developing data science and machine learning applications, you have to know what the field of data science and machine learning is, what you can do with that, and what are some of the best tools and libraries that you can use. The first chapter of the book answers these questions.

2. Learn a Programming Language

If you wish to be a data science and machine learning expert, you have to learn programming. There is no working around this fact. Though there are several cloud-based machine learning platforms like Amazon Sage Maker and Azure ML Studio where you can create data science applications without writing a single line of code. However, to get fine-grained control over your applications, you will need to learn programming.

And though you can program natural language applications in any programming language, I would recommend that you learn Python programming language. Python is one of the most routinely used libraries for data science and machine learning with myriads of basic and advanced data science and ML libraries. In addition, many data science applications are based on deep learning and machine learning techniques. Again, Python is the language that provides easy to use libraries for deep learning and machine learning. In short, learn Python. Chapter 2 contains a crash course for absolute beginners in Python.

3. Start with the Basics

Start with very basic data science applications. I would rather recommend that you should not start developing data science applications right away. Start with basic mathematical and numerical operations like computing dot products and matrix multiplication, etc. Chapter 3 of this book explains how to use the NumPy library for basic data science and machine learning tasks. You should also know how to import data into your application and how to visualize it. Chapters 4 and 5 of this book explain the task of data analysis and visualization. After that, you should know how to visualize and preprocess data.

4. Learn Machine Learning and Deep Learning Algorithms

Data Science, machine learning, and deep learning go hand in hand. Therefore, you have to learn machine learning and deep learning algorithms. Among machine learning, start with the supervised learning techniques. Supervised machine learning algorithms are chiefly divided into two types, i.e., regression and classification. Chapter 6 of this book explains regression algorithms, while chapter 7 explains classification algorithms. Chapter 8 explains unsupervised machine learning, while chapter 9 briefly reviews deep learning techniques. Finally, the 10th Chapter explains how to reduce feature (dimensions) set to improve the performance of machine learning applications.

5. Develop Data Science Applications

Once you are familiar with basic machine learning and deep learning algorithms, you are good to go for developing data science applications. Data science applications can be of different types, i.e., predicting house prices, recognizing images, classifying text, etc. Being a beginner, you should try to develop versatile data science applications, and later, when you find your area of interest, e.g., natural language processing or image recognition, delve deep into that. It is important to mention that this book provides a very generic introduction to data science, and you will see applications of data science to structured data, textual data, and image data. However, this book is not dedicated to any specific data science field.

6. Deploying Data Science Applications

To put a data science or machine learning application into production so that anyone can use it, you need to deploy it to production. There are several ways to deploy data science applications. You can use dedicated servers containing REST APIs that can be used to call various functionalities in your data science application. To deploy such applications, you need to learn Python Flask, Docker, or similar web technology. In addition to that, you can also deploy your applications using Amazon Web Services or any other cloud-based deployment platform.

To be an expert data science and machine learning practitioner, you need to perform the aforementioned 6 steps in an iterative manner. The more you practice, the better you will get at NLP.

1.3. Environment Setup

1.3.1. Windows Setup

The time has come to install Python on Windows using an IDE. In fact, we will use Anaconda throughout this book right from installing Python to writing multi-threaded codes in the coming lectures. Now, let us get going with the installation.

This section explains how you can download and install Anaconda on Windows.

Follow these steps to download and install Anaconda.

1. Open the following URL in your browser:

    https://www.anaconda.com/distribution/

2. The browser will take you to the following webpage. Select the latest version of Python (3.7 at the time of writing this book). Now, click the **Download** button to download the executable file. Depending upon the speed of your internet, the file will download within 2–3 minutes.

3. Run the executable file after the download is complete. You will most likely find the download file in your download folder. The name of the file should be similar to "Anaconda3-5.1.0-Windows-x86_64." The installation wizard will open when you run the file, as shown in the following figure. Click the **Next** button.

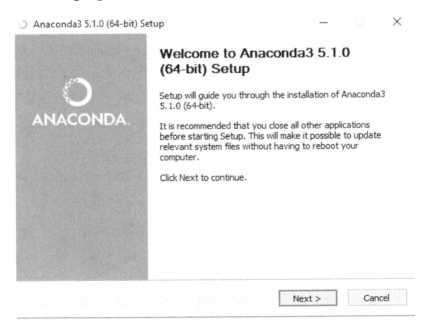

4. Now, click **I Agree** on the *License Agreement* dialog, as shown in the following screenshot.

5. Check the *Just Me* radio button from the *Select Installation Type* dialogue box. Click the **Next** button to continue.

6. Now, the *Choose Install Location* dialog will be displayed. Change the directory if you want, but the default is preferred. The installation folder should at least have 3 GB of free space for Anaconda. Click the **Next** button.

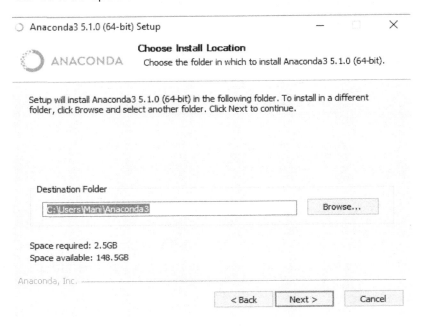

7. Go for the second option, *Register Anaconda as my default Python 3.7* in the *Advanced Installation Options* dialogue box. Click the **Install** button to start the installation, which can take some time to complete.

○ Anaconda3 5.1.0 (64-bit) Setup — □ ✕

ANACONDA

Advanced Installation Options
Customize how Anaconda integrates with Windows

Advanced Options

☐ Add Anaconda to my PATH environment variable

Not recommended. Instead, open Anaconda with the Windows Start
menu and select "Anaconda (64-bit)". This "add to PATH" option makes
Anaconda get found before previously installed software, but may
cause problems requiring you to uninstall and reinstall Anaconda.

☑ Register Anaconda as my default Python 3.6

This will allow other programs, such as Python Tools for Visual Studio
PyCharm, Wing IDE, PyDev, and MSI binary packages, to automatically
detect Anaconda as the primary Python 3.6 on the system.

Anaconda, Inc.

[< Back] [**Install**] [Cancel]

8. Click **Next** once the installation is complete.

○ Anaconda3 5.1.0 (64-bit) Setup — □

ANACONDA

Installation Complete
Setup was completed successfully.

Completed

[Show details]

Anaconda, Inc.

[< Back] [**Next >**] [Cancel]

9. Click **Skip** on the *Microsoft Visual Studio Code Installation* dialog box.

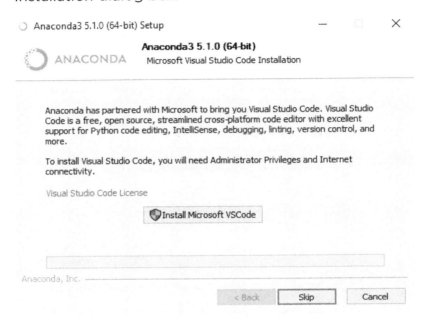

10. You have successfully installed Anaconda on your Windows. Excellent job. The next step is to uncheck both checkboxes on the dialog box. Now, click on the **Finish** button.

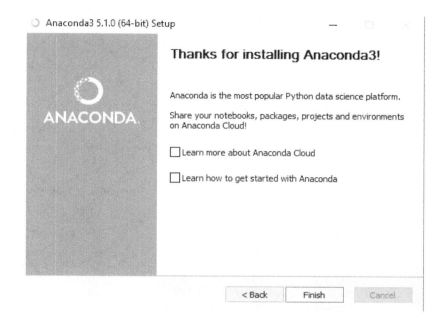

1.3.2. Mac Setup

Anaconda's installation process is almost the same for Mac. It may differ graphically, but you will follow the same steps you followed for Windows. The only difference is that you have to download the executable file, which is compatible with the Mac operating system.

This section explains how you can download and install Anaconda on Mac.

Follow these steps to download and install Anaconda.

1. Open the following URL in your browser:

   https://www.anaconda.com/distribution/

2. The browser will take you to the following webpage. Select the latest version of Python for Mac (3.7 at the time of writing this book). Now, click the **Download**

button to download the executable file. Depending upon the speed of your internet, the file will download within 2–3 minutes.

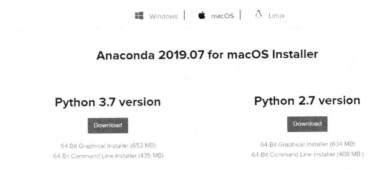

3. Run the executable file after the download is complete. You will most likely find the download file in your download folder. The name of the file should be similar to "Anaconda3-5.1.0-Windows-x86_64." The installation wizard will open when you run the file, as shown in the following figure. Click the **Continue** button.

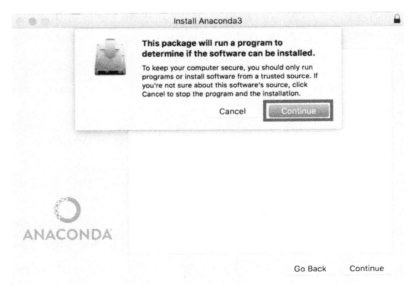

4. Now click **Continue** on the *Welcome to Anaconda 3 Installer* window, as shown in the following screenshot.

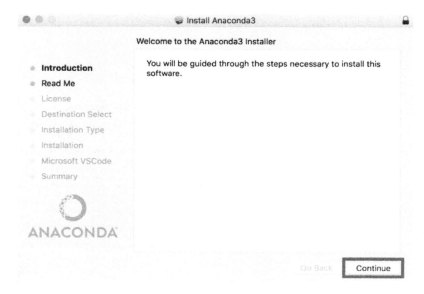

5. The *Important Information* dialog will pop up. Simply click **Continue** to go with the default version that is Anaconda 3.

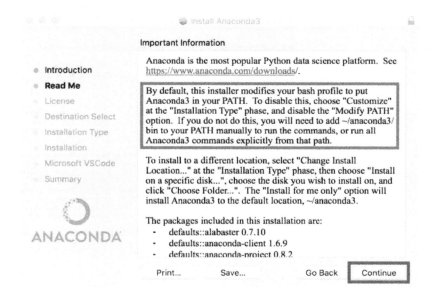

6. Click **Continue** on the *Software License Agreement* Dialog.

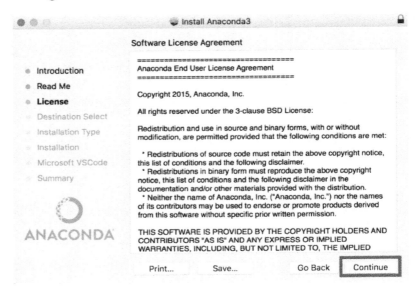

7. It is mandatory to read the license agreement and click the **Agree** button before you can click the **Continue** button again.

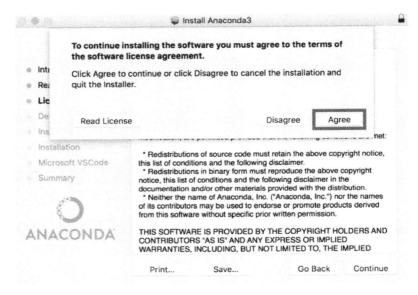

8. Simply click **Install** on the next window that appears.

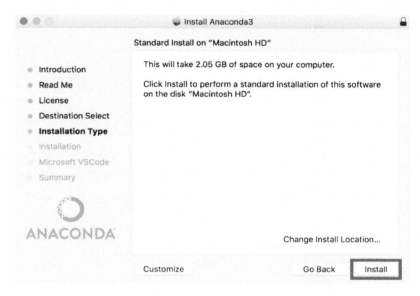

The system will prompt you to give your password. Use the same password you use to login to your Mac computer. Now, click on **Install Software**.

9. Click **Continue** on the next window. You also have the option to install Microsoft VSCode at this point.

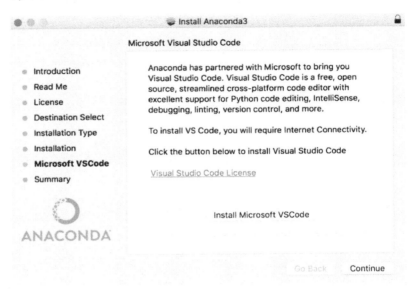

The next screen will display the message that the installation has completed successfully. Click on the **Close** button to close the installer.

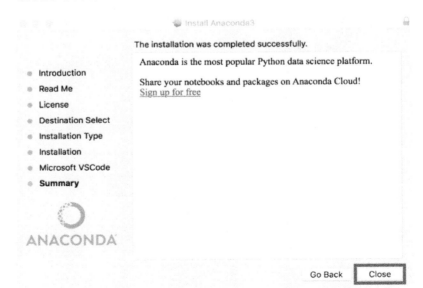

There you have it. You have successfully installed Anaconda on your Mac computer. Now, you can write Python code in Jupyter and Spyder the same way you wrote it in Windows.

1.3.3. Linux Setup

We have used Python's graphical installers for installation on Windows and Mac. However, we will use the command line to install Python on Ubuntu or Linux. Linux is also more resource-friendly, and the installation of software is particularly easy as well.

Follow these steps to install Anaconda on Linux (Ubuntu distribution).

1. Go to the following link to copy the installer bash script from the latest available version:

   https://www.anaconda.com/distribution/

   Windows | macOS | Linux

   Anaconda 2019.07 for Linux Installer

   Python 3.7 version   **Python 2.7 version**

   Download   Download

   64-Bit (x86) Installer (517 MB)   64-Bit (x86) Installer (476 MB)
   64-Bit (Power8 and Power9) Installer (326 MB)   64-Bit (Power8 and Power9) Installer (298 MB)

2. The second step is to download the installer bash script. Log into your Linux computer and open your terminal. Now, go to /temp directory and download the bash you downloaded from Anaconda's home page using curl.

```
$ cd / tmp

$ curl -o https://repo.anaconda.com.archive/Anaconda3-
5.2.0-Linux-x86_64.sh
```

3. You should also use the cryptographic hash verification through SHA-256 checksum to verify the integrity of the installer.

```
$ sha256sum Anaconda3-5.2.0-Linux-x86_64.sh
```

You will get the following output.

```
09f53738b0cd3bb96f5b1bac488e5528df9906be2480fe61df40e0e
0d19e3d48 Anaconda3-5.2.0-Linux-x86_64.sh
```

4. The fourth step is to run the Anaconda Script as shown in the following figure.

```
$ bash Anaconda3-5.2.0-Linux-x86_64.sh
```

The command line will produce the following output. You will be asked to review the license agreement. Keep on pressing **Enter** until you reach the end.

```
Output

Welcome to Anaconda3 5.2.0

In order to continue the installation process, please
review the license agreement.
Please, press Enter to continue
>>>
...
Do you approve the license terms? [yes|No]
```

Type *Yes* when you get to the bottom of the License Agreement.

5. The installer will ask you to choose the installation location after you agree to the license agreement.

Simply press **Enter** to choose the default location. You can also specify a different location if you want.

```
Output

Anaconda3 will now be installed on this location:
/home/tola/anaconda3

- Press ENTER to confirm the location
- Press CTRL-C to abort the installation
- Or specify a different location below

[/home/tola/anaconda3] >>>
```

The installation will proceed once you press **Enter**. Once again, you have to be patient as the installation process takes some time to complete.

6. You will receive the following result when the installation is complete. If you wish to use conda command, type *Yes*.

```
Output
...
Installation finished.
Do you wish the installer to prepend Anaconda3 install
location to path in your /home/tola/.bashrc? [yes|no]
[no]>>>
```

At this point, you will also have the option to download the Visual Studio Code. Type *yes* or *no* to install or decline, respectively.

7. Use the following command to activate your brand-new installation of Anaconda3.

```
$ source `/.bashrc
```

8. You can also test the installation using the conda command.

```
$ conda list
```

Congratulations. You have successfully installed Anaconda on your Linux system.

1.3.4. Using Google Colab Cloud Environment

In addition to local Python environments such as Anaconda, you can run deep learning applications on Google Colab as well, which is Google's platform for deep learning with GPU support. All the codes in this book have been run using Google Colab. Therefore, I would suggest that you use Google Colab, too.

To run deep learning applications via Google Colab, all you need is a Google/Gmail account. Once you have a Google/Gmail account, you can simply go to:

https://colab.research.google.com/

Next, click on File -> New notebook, as shown in the following screenshot:

Next, to run your code using GPU, from the top menu, select Runtime -> Change runtime type, as shown in the following screenshot:

Runtime Tools Help Last edited on M

Run all	Ctrl+F9
Run before	Ctrl+F8
Run the focused cell	Ctrl+Enter
Run selection	Ctrl+Shift+Enter
Run after	Ctrl+F10

Factory reset runtime

Change runtime type

Manage sessions

You should see the following window. Here, from the dropdown list, select GPU, and click the **Save** button.

Notebook settings

Runtime type
Python 3

Hardware accelerator
GPU ?

To get the most out of Colab, avoid using a GPU unless you need one. Learn more

☐ Omit code cell output when saving this notebook

CANCEL   SAVE

To make sure you are running the latest version of TensorFlow, execute the following script in the Google Colab notebook cell. The following script will update your TensorFlow version.

```
pip install --upgrade tensorflow
```

To check if you are really running TensorFlow version > 2.0, execute the following script.

```
1.    import tensorflow as tf
2.    print(tf.__version__)
```

With Google Cloud, you can import the datasets from your Google drive. Execute the following script. And click on the link that appears as shown below:

```
from google.colab import drive
drive.mount('/gdrive')

Go to this URL in a browser: https://accounts.google.com/o/oauth2/auth

Enter your authorization code:
```

You will be prompted to allow Google Colab to access your Google drive. Click the **Allow** button, as shown below:

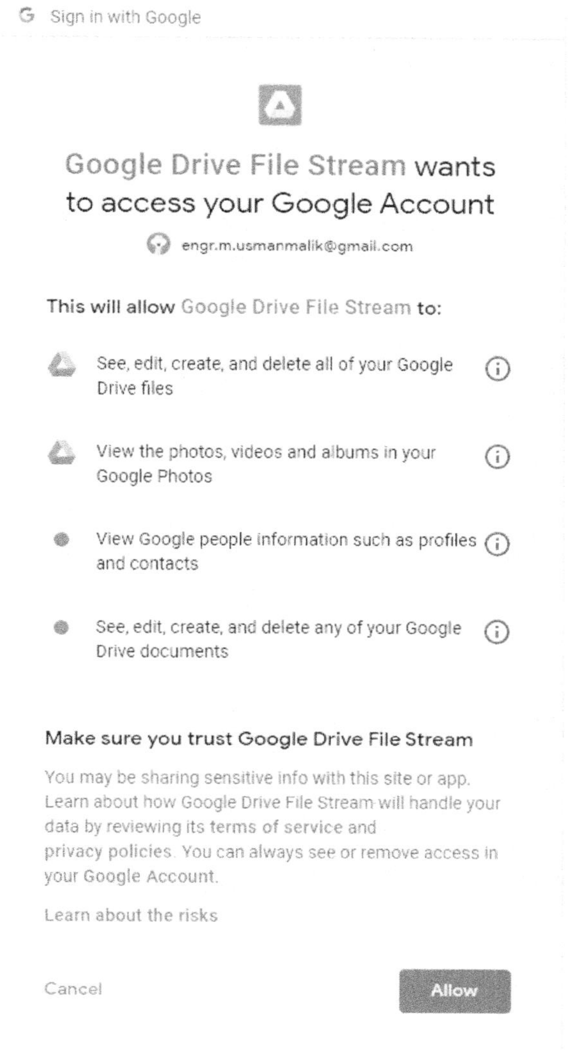

G   Sign in with Google

Google Drive File Stream wants
to access your Google Account

engr.m.usmanmalik@gmail.com

This will allow Google Drive File Stream to:

See, edit, create, and delete all of your Google
Drive files

View the photos, videos and albums in your
Google Photos

View Google people information such as profiles
and contacts

See, edit, create, and delete any of your Google
Drive documents

Make sure you trust Google Drive File Stream

You may be sharing sensitive info with this site or app.
Learn about how Google Drive File Stream will handle your
data by reviewing its terms of service and
privacy policies. You can always see or remove access in
your Google Account.

Learn about the risks

Cancel   Allow

You will see a link appear, as shown in the following image (the link has been blinded here).

Sign in

Please copy this code, switch to your application and paste it there:

cIjiqzw

Copy the link and paste it in the empty field in the Google Colab cell, as shown below:

```
from google.colab import drive
drive.mount('/gdrive')

Go to this URL in a browser: https://accounts.google.com/o/oauth2/auth

Enter your authorization code:
```

This way, you can import datasets from your Google drive to your Google Colab environment.

In the next chapter, you will see how to write your first program in Python, along with other Python programming concepts.

2

Python Crash Course

If you are familiar with the basic concepts of the Python programming language, you can skip this chapter. For those who are absolute beginners to Python, this section provides a very brief overview of some of the most basic concepts of Python. Python is a very vast programming language, and this section is by no means a substitute for a complete Python book. However, if you want to see how various operations and commands are executed in Python, you are welcome to follow along the rest of this section.

2.1. Writing Your First Program

You have already installed Python on your computer and established a unique environment in the form of Anaconda. Now, it is time to write your first program, that is the Hello World!

In order to write a program in Anaconda, you have to launch Anaconda Navigator. Search *Anaconda Navigator* in your Windows Search Box. Now, click on the *Anaconda Navigator* application icon, as shown in the following figure.

Once you click on the application, the Anaconda's Dashboard will open. The dashboard offers you a myriad of tools to write your code. We will use *Jupyter Notebook*, the most popular of these tools, to write and explain the code throughout this book.

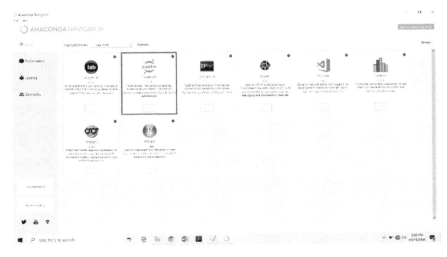

The Jupyter Notebook is available at second from the top of the dashboard. You can use Jupyter Notebook even if you don't have access to the internet, as it runs right in your default browser. Another method to open Jupyter Notebook is to type Jupyter Notebook in the Windows search bar. Subsequently, click on the Jupyter Notebook application. The application will open in a new tab on your browser.

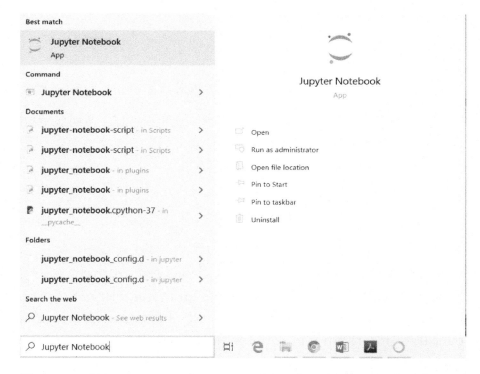

The top right corner of Jupyter Notebook's own dashboard houses a *New* button, which you have to click to open a new document. A dropdown containing several options will appear. Click on *Python 3*.

A new Python notebook will appear for you to write your programs. It looks as follows:

Jupyter Notebook consists of cells, as evident from the above image, making its layout very simple and straightforward. You will write your code inside these cells. Let us write our first ever Python program in Jupyter Notebook.

Script 1:

1.3.1. Writing Your First Program

```
In [1]:  print("Welcome to Data Visualization with Python")

         Welcome to Data Visualization with Python
```

The above script basically prints a string value in the output using the **print()** method. The **print()** method is used to print on the console, any string passed to it. If you see the following output, you have successfully run your first Python program.

Output:

```
Welcome to Data Visualization with Python
```

Let's now explore some of the other important Python concepts starting with Variables and Data Types.

Requirements – Anaconda, Jupyter, and Matplotlib

- Every script in this book has been executed via Jupyter Notebook. Therefore, you should have Jupyter Notebook installed.
- It goes without saying that we will be using the Matplotlib library.
- The Numpy and Pandas libraries should also be installed before this chapter.

Hands-on Time – Source Codes

All IPython notebooks for the source code of all the scripts in this chapter can be found in the *Source Codes/Chapter 2* folder in the GitHub repository. I would suggest that you write all the code in this chapter yourself and see if you can get the same output as mentioned in this chapter.

2.2. Python Variables and Data Types

Data types in a programming language refer to the type of data that the language is capable of processing. The following are the major data types supported by Python:

a. Strings

b. Integers

c. Floating Point Numbers

d. Booleans

e. Lists

f. Tuples

g. Dictionaries

A variable is an alias for the memory address where actual data is stored. The data or the values stored at a memory address can be accessed and updated via the variable name. Unlike other programming languages like C++, Java, and C#, Python is loosely typed, which means that you don't have to define the data type while creating a variable. Rather, the type of data is evaluated at runtime.

The following example demonstrates how to create different data types and how to store them in their corresponding variables. The script also prints the type of the variables via the **type()** function.

Script 2:

```
1.  # A string Variable
2.  first_name = "Joseph"
3.  print(type(first_name))
4.
5.  # An Integer Variable
6.  age = 20
7.  print(type(age))
8.
9.  # A floating point variable
10. weight = 70.35
11. print(type(weight))
12.
13. # A floating point variable
14. married = False
15. print(type(married))
16.
17. #List
```

```
18. cars = ["Honda", "Toyota", "Suzuki"]
19. print(type(cars))
20.
21. #Tuples
22. days = ("Sunday", "Monday", "Tuesday", "Wednesday",
    "Thursday", "Friday", "Saturday")
23. print(type(days))
24.
25. #Dictionaries
26. days2 = {1:"Sunday", 2:"Monday", 3:"Tuesday", 4:"Wednesday",
    5:"Thursday", 6:"Friday", 7:"Saturday"}
27. print(type(days2))
```

Output:

```
<class 'str'>
<class 'int'>
<class 'float'>
<class 'bool'>
<class 'list'>
<class 'tuple'>
<class 'dict'>
```

2.3. Python Operators

Python programming language contains the following types of operators:

    a. Arithmetic Operators

    b. Logical Operators

    c. Comparison Operators

    d. Assignment Operators

    e. Membership Operators

Let's briefly review each of these types of operators.

§ Arithmetic Operators

Arithmetic operators are used to perform arithmetic operations in Python. The following table sums up the arithmetic operators supported by Python. Suppose X = 20, and Y = 10.

Operator Name	Symbol	Functionality	Example
Addition	+	Adds the operands on either side	X+ Y= 30
Subtraction	−	Subtracts the operands on either side	X −Y= 10
Multiplication	*	Multiplies the operands on either side	X * Y= 200
Division	/	Divides the operand on the left by the one on the right	X / Y= 2.0
Modulus	%	Divides the operand on the left by the one on the right and returns the remainder	X % Y= 0
Exponent	**	Takes exponent of the operand on the left to the power of right	X ** Y = $1024 \times e^{10}$

Here is an example of arithmetic operators with output:

Script 3:

```
1.  X = 20
2.  Y = 10
3.  print(X + Y)
4.  print(X - Y)
5.  print(X * Y)
6.  print(X / Y)
7.  print(X ** Y)
```

Output:

```
30
10
200
2.0
10240000000000
```

§ Logical Operators

Logical operators are used to perform logical **AND, OR**, and **NOT** operations in Python. The following table summarizes the logical operators. Here, **X** is **True,** and **Y** is **False**.

Operator	Symbol	Functionality	Example
Logical AND	and	If both the operands are true, then the condition becomes true.	(X and Y) = False
Logical OR	or	If any of the two operands are true, then the condition becomes true.	(X or Y) = True
Logical NOT	not	Used to reverse the logical state of its operand.	not(X and Y) =True

Here is an example that explains the usage of Python logical operators.

Script 4:

```
1.  X = True
2.  Y = False
3.  print(X and Y)
4.  print(X or Y)
5.  print(not(X and Y))
```

Output:

```
1.  False
2.  True
3.  True
```

§ Comparison Operators

Comparison operators, as the name suggests, are used to compare two or more than two operands. Depending upon the relation between the operands, comparison operators return Boolean values. The following table summarizes comparison operators in Python. Here, X is 20, and Y is 35.

Operator	Symbol	Description	Example
Equality	==	Returns true if values of both the operands are equal	(X == Y) = false
Inequality	!=	Returns true if values of both the operands are not equal	(X = Y) = true
Greater than	>	Returns true if value of the left operand is greater than the right one	(X> Y) = False
Smaller than	<	Returns true if the value of the left operand is smaller than the right one	(X< Y) = True
Greater than or equal to	>=	Returns true if value of the left operand is greater than or equal to the right one	(X > =Y) = False
Smaller than or equal to	<=	Returns true if the value of the left operand is smaller than or equal to the right one	(X<= Y) = True

The comparison operators have been demonstrated in action in the following example:

Script 5

```
1.  X = 20
2.  Y = 35
3.
4.  print(X == Y)
5.  print(X != Y)
6.  print(X > Y)
7.  print(X < Y)
8.  print(X >= Y)
9.  print(X <= Y)
```

Output:

```
False
True
False
True
False
True
```

§ Assignment Operators

Assignment operators are used to assign values to variables. The following table summarizes the assignment operators. Here, X is 20, and Y is equal to 10.

Operator	Symbol	Description	Example
Assignment	=	Used to assign the value of the right operand to the right.	R = X+ Y assigns 30 to R
Add and assign	+=	Adds the operands on either side and assigns the result to the left operand	X += Y assigns 30 to X
Subtract and assign	-=	Subtracts the operands on either side and assigns the result to the left operand	X -= Y assigns 10 to X

Multiply and Assign	*=	Multiplies the operands on either side and assigns the result to the left operand	X *= Y assigns 200 to X
Divide and Assign	/=	Divides the operands on the left by the right and assigns the result to the left operand	X /= Y assigns 2 to X
Take modulus and assign	%=	Divides the operands on the left by the right and assigns the remainder to the left operand	X %= Y assigns 0 to X
Take exponent and assign	**=	Takes exponent of the operand on the left to the power of right and assigns the remainder to the left operand	X **= Y assigns 1024 x e^{10} to X

Take a look at script 6 to see Python assignment operators in action.

Script 6:

```
1.  X = 20; Y = 10
2.  R = X + Y
3.  print(R)
4.
5.  X = 20;
6.  Y = 10
7.  X += Y
8.  print(X)
9.
10. X = 20;
11. Y = 10
12. X -= Y
13. print(X)
14.
15. X = 20;
16. Y = 10
```

```
17. X *= Y
18. print(X)
19.
20. X = 20;
21. Y = 10
22. X /= Y
23. print(X)
24.
25. X = 20;
26. Y = 10
27. X %= Y
28. print(X)
29.
30. X = 20;
31. Y = 10
32. X **= Y
33. print(X)
```

Output:

```
30
30
10
200
2.0
0
10240000000000
```

§ Membership Operators

Membership operators are used to find if an item is a member of a collection of items or not. There are two types of membership operators: the **in** operator and the **not in** operator. The following script shows the **in** operator in action.

Script 7:

```
1.  days = ("Sunday", "Monday", "Tuesday", "Wednesday",
     "Thursday", "Friday", "Saturday")
2.  print('Sunday' in days)
```

Output:

```
True
```

And here is an example of the **not in** operator.

Script 8:

```
1.  days = ("Sunday", "Monday", "Tuesday", "Wednesday",
    "Thursday", "Friday", "Saturday")
2.  print('Xunday' not in days)
```

Output:

```
True
```

2.4. Conditional Statements

Conditional statements in Python are used to implement conditional logic in Python. Conditional statements help you decide whether to execute a certain code block or not. There are three main types of conditional statements in Python:

    a. If statement

    b. If-else statement

    c. If-elif statement

§ IF Statement

If you have to check for a single condition and you do not concern about the alternate condition, you can use the **if** statement. For instance, if you want to check if 10 is greater than 5 and based on that you want to print a statement, you can use the if statement. The condition evaluated by the **if** statement returns a Boolean value. If the condition evaluated by the **if** statement is true, the code block that follows the **if** statement executes. It is important to mention that in Python, a new code block starts at a new line with on tab indented from the left when compared with the outer block.

Here, in the following example, the condition 10 > 5 is evaluated, which returns true. Hence, the code block that follows the **if** statement executes, and a message is printed on the console.

Script 9:

```
1.  # The if statement
2.
3.  if 10 > 5:
4.      print("Ten is greater than 10")
```

Output:

```
Ten is greater than 10
```

§ IF-Else Statement

The **If-else** statement comes handy when you want to execute an alternate piece of code in case the condition for the if statement returns false. For instance, in the following example, the condition 5 < 10 will return false. Hence, the code block that follows the **else** statement will execute.

Script 10:

```
1.  # if-else statement
2.
3.  if  5 > 10:
4.      print("5 is greater than 10")
5.  else:
6.      print("10 is greater than 5")
```

Output:

```
10 is greater than 5
```

§ IF-Elif Statement

The **if-elif** statement comes handy when you have to evaluate multiple conditions. For instance, in the following example, we first check if 5 > 10, which evaluates to false. Next, an **elif** statement evaluates the condition 8 < 4, which also returns false. Hence, the code block that follows the last **else** statement executes.

Script 11:

```
1. #if-elif and else
2.
3. if  5 > 10:
4.     print("5 is greater than 10")
5. elif 8 < 4:
6.     print("8 is smaller than 4")
7. else:
8.     print("5 is not greater than 10 and 8 is not smaller
    than 4")
```

Output:

```
5   is not greater than 10 and 8 is not smaller than 4
```

2.5. Iteration Statements

Iteration statements, also known as loops, are used to iteratively execute a certain piece of code. There are two main types of iteration statements in Python:

a. For loop

b. While Loop

§ For Loop

The **for loop** is used to iteratively execute a piece of code for a certain number of times. You should typically use **for loop** when you know the exact number of iterations or repetitions for which you want to run your code. A **for loop** iterates over a collection of items. In the following example, we create a collection of five integers using the **range()** method. Next, a **for loop** iterates five times and prints each integer in the collection.

Script 12:

```
1. items = range(5)
2. for item in items:
3.     print(item)
```

Output:

```
0
1
2
3
4
```

§ While Loop

The **while loop** keeps executing a certain piece of code unless the evaluation condition becomes false. For instance, the **while loop** in the following script keeps executing unless the variable c becomes greater than 10.

Script 13:

```
1. c = 0
2. while c < 10:
3.     print(c)
4.     c = c +1
```

Output:

```
0
1
2
3
4
```

```
5
6
7
8
9
```

2.6. Functions

In any programming language, functions are used to implement the piece of code that is required to be executed numerous times at different locations in the code. In such cases, instead of writing long pieces of codes again and again, you can simply define a function that contains the piece of code, and then you can call the function wherever you want in the code.

To create a function in Python, the *def* keyword is used, followed by the name of the function and opening and closing parenthesis.

Once a function is defined, you have to call it in order to execute the code inside a function body. To call a function, you simply have to specify the name of the function, followed by opening and closing parenthesis. In the following script, we create a function named **myfunc**, which prints a simple statement on the console using the **print()** method.

Script 14:

```
1.  def myfunc():
2.      print("This is a simple function")
3.
4.  ### function call
5.  myfunc()
```

Output:

```
This is a simple function
```

You can also pass values to a function. The values are passed inside the parenthesis of the function call. However, you must specify the parameter name in the function definition, too. In the following script, we define a function named **myfuncparam()**. The function accepts one parameter, i.e., **num**. The value passed in the parenthesis of the function call will be stored in this **num** variable and will be printed by the **print()**method inside the **myfuncparam()** method.

Script 15:

```
1.  def myfuncparam(num):
2.      print("This is a function with parameter value: "+num)
3.
4.  ### function call
5.  myfuncparam("Parameter 1")
```

Output:

```
This is a function with parameter value:Parameter 1
```

Finally, a function can also return values to the function call. To do so, you simply have to use the return keyword, followed by the value that you want to return. In the following script, the **myreturnfunc()** function returns a string value to the calling function.

Script 16:

```
1.  def myreturnfunc():
2.      return "This function returns a value"
3.
4.  val = myreturnfunc()
5.  print(val)
```

Output:

```
This function returns a value
```

2.7. Objects and Classes

Python supports object-oriented programming (OOP). In OOP, any entity that can perform some function and have some attributes is implemented in the form of an object.

For instance, a car can be implemented as an object since a car has some attributes such as price, color, model, and can perform some functions such as drive car, change gear, stop car, etc.

Similarly, a fruit can also be implemented as an object since a fruit has a price, name, and you can eat a fruit, grow a fruit, and perform functions with a fruit.

To create an object, you first have to define a class. For instance, in the following example, a class **Fruit** has been defined. The class has two attributes, **name** and **price**, and one method, **eat_fruit()**. Next, we create an object **f** of class Fruit and then call the **eat_fruit()** method from the **f** object. We also access the **name** and **price** attributes of the **f** object and print them on the console.

Script 17:

```
1.  class Fruit:
2.
3.      name = "apple"
4.      price = 10
5.
6.      def eat_fruit(self):
7.          print("Fruit has been eaten")
8.
9.
10. f = Fruit()
11. f.eat_fruit()
12. print(f.name)
13. print(f.price)
```

Output:

```
Fruit has been eaten
apple
10
```

A class in Python can have a special method called a *constructor*. The name of the constructor method in Python is **__init__()**. The constructor is called whenever an object of a class is created. Look at the following example to see the constructor in action.

Script 18:

```
1.  class Fruit:
2.
3.      name = "apple"
4.      price = 10
5.
6.      def __init__(self, fruit_name, fruit_price):
7.          Fruit.name = fruit_name
8.          Fruit.price = fruit_price
9.
10.     def eat_fruit(self):
11.         print("Fruit has been eaten")
12.
13.
14. f = Fruit("Orange", 15)
15. f.eat_fruit()
16. print(f.name)
17. print(f.price)
```

Output:

```
Fruit has been eaten
Orange
15
```

2.8. Data Science and Machine Learning Libraries

Owing to the growing importance of data science and machine learning techniques, several Python libraries have been developed. Some of these libraries have been briefly reviewed in this section.

2.8.1. NumPy

NumPy is one of the most commonly used libraries for numeric and scientific computing. NumPy is extremely fast and contains support for multiple mathematical domains such as linear algebra, geometry, etc. It is extremely important to learn NumPy in case you plan to make a career in data science and data preparation.

To know more about NumPy, check this link:

https://numpy.org/

2.8.2. Matplotlib

Matplotlib is the de facto standard for static data visualization in Python, which is the first step in data science and machine learning. Being the oldest data visualization library in Python, Matplotlib is the most widely used data visualization library. Matplotlib was developed to resemble MATLAB, which is one of the most widely used programming languages in academia.

While Matplotlib graphs are easy to plot, the look and feel of the Matplotlib plots have a distinct feel of the 1990s. Many wrappers libraries like Pandas and Seaborn have been developed on top of Matplotlib. These libraries allow users to plot much cleaner and sophisticated graphs.

To study more about Matplotlib, check this link:

https://matplotlib.org/

2.8.3. Seaborn

Seaborn library is built on top of the Matplotlib library and contains all the plotting capabilities of Matplotlib. However, with Seaborn, you can plot much more pleasing and aesthetic graphs with the help of Seaborn default styles and color palettes.

To study more about Seaborn, check this link:

https://seaborn.pydata.org/

2.8.4. Pandas

Pandas library, like Seaborn, is based on the Matplotlib library and offers utilities that can be used to plot different types of static plots in a single line of codes. With Pandas, you can import data in various formats such as CSV (Comma Separated View) and TSV (Tab Separated View) and can plot a variety of data visualizations via these data sources.

To know more about Seaborn, check this link:

https://pandas.pydata.org/

2.8.5. Scikit Learn

Scikit Learn, also called sklearn, is an extremely useful library for data science and machine learning in Python. Sklearn contains many built-in modules that can be used to perform data preparation tasks such as feature engineering, feature scaling, outlier detection, discretization, etc. You will be using Sklearn a lot in this book. Therefore, it can be a good idea to study sklearn before you start coding using this book.

To study more about Scikit Learn, check this link:

https://scikit-learn.org/stable/

2.8.6. TensorFlow

TensorFlow is one of the most frequently used libraries for deep learning. TensorFlow has been developed by Google and offers an easy to use API for the development of various deep learning models. TensorFlow is consistently being updated, and at the time of writing of this book, TensorFlow 2 is the latest major release of TensorFlow. With TensorFlow, you can not only easily develop deep learning applications but also deploy them with ease owing to the deployment functionalities of TensorFlow.

To study more about TensorFlow, check this link:

https://www.tensorflow.org/

2.8.7. Keras

Keras is a high-level TensorFlow library that implements complex TensorFlow functionalities under the hood. If you are a newbie to deep learning, Keras is the one deep learning library that you should start for developing deep learning library. As a matter of fact, Keras has been adopted as the official deep learning library for TensorFlow 2.0, and now all the TensorFlow applications use Keras abstractions for training deep learning models.

To study more about Keras, check this link:

https://keras.io/

Hands-on Time – Exercise
Now, it is your turn. Follow the instructions in **the exercises below** to check your understanding of the advanced data visualization with Matplotlib. The answers to these exercises are provided after chapter 10 in this book.

Exercise 2.1

Question 1

Which iteration should be used when you want to repeatedly execute a code for a specific number of times?

    A. For Loop

    B. While Loop

    C. Both A and B

    D. None of the above

Question 2

What is the maximum number of values that a function can return in Python?

    A. Single Value

    B. Double Value

    C. More than two values

    D. None

Question 3

Which of the following membership operators are supported by Python?

    A. In

    B. Out

    C. Not In

    D. Both A and C

Exercise 2.2

Print the table of integer 9 using a while loop:

Python NumPy Library for Data Analysis

NumPy (Numerical Python) is a Python library for data science and numerical computing. Many advanced data science and machine learning libraries require data to be in the form of NumPy arrays before it can be processed. In this chapter, you are going to learn some of the most commonly used functionalities of the NumPy array. NumPy comes prebuilt with Anaconda's distribution of Python. Or else, you can install NumPy with the following pip command in a terminal or a command prompt:

```
$ pip install numpy
```

3.1. Advantages of NumPy Library

A NumPy array has many advantages over regular Python lists. Some of them are listed below:

1. NumPy arrays are much faster for insertion, deletion, updating, and reading of data.

2. NumPy arrays contain advanced broadcasting functionalities compared with regular Python arrays.

3. NumPy array comes with a lot of methods that support advanced arithmetic and linear algebra options.

4. NumPy provides advanced multi-dimensional array slicing capabilities.

In the next section, you will see how to create NumPy arrays using different methods.

3.2. Creating NumPy Arrays

Depending upon the type of data you need inside your NumPy array, different methods can be used to create a NumPy array.

3.2.1. Using Array Methods

To create a NumPy array, you can pass a list to the **array()** method of the NumPy module as shown below:

Script 1:

```
1. import numpy as np
2. nums_list = [10,12,14,16,20]
3. nums_array = np.array(nums_list)
4. type(nums_array)
```

Output:

```
numpy.ndarray
```

You can also create a multi-dimensional NumPy array. To do so, you need to create a list of lists where each internal list corresponds to the row in a 2-dimensional array. Here is an example of how to create a 2-dimensional array using the **array()** method.

Script 2:

```
1.  row1 = [10,12,13]
2.  row2 = [45,32,16]
3.  row3 = [45,32,16]
4.
5.  nums_2d = np.array([row1, row2, row3])
6.  nums_2d.shape
```

Output:

```
(3, 3)
```

3.2.2. Using Arrange Method

With the **arrange ()** method, you can create a NumPy array that contains a range of integers. The first parameter to the arrange method is the lower bound, and the second parameter is the upper bound. The lower bound is included in the array. However, the upper bound is not included. The following script creates a NumPy array with integers 5 to 10.

Script 3:

```
1.  nums_arr = np.arange(5,11)
2.  print(nums_arr)
```

Output:

```
[ 5  6  7  8  9 10]
```

You can also specify the step as a third parameter in the **arrange()** function. A step defines the distance between two consecutive points in the array. The following script creates a NumPy array from 5 to 11 with a step size of 2.

Script 4:

```
1.  nums_arr = np.arange(5,12,2)
2.  print(nums_arr)
```

Output:

```
[ 5   7   9 11]
```

3.2.3. Using Ones Method

The **ones()** method can be used to create a NumPy array of all ones. Here is an example.

Script 5:

```
1.  ones_array = np.ones(6)
2.  print(ones_array)
```

Output:

```
[1. 1. 1. 1. 1. 1.]
```

You can create a 2-dimensional array of all ones by passing the number of rows and columns as the first and second parameters of the **ones()** method, as shown below:

Script 6:

```
1.  ones_array = np.ones((6,4))
2.  print(ones_array)
```

Output:

```
[[1. 1. 1. 1.]
 [1. 1. 1. 1.]
 [1. 1. 1. 1.]
 [1. 1. 1. 1.]
 [1. 1. 1. 1.]
 [1. 1. 1. 1.]]
```

3.2.4. Using Zeros Method

The **zeros()** method can be used to create a NumPy array of all zeros. Here is an example.

Script 7:

```
1. zeros_array = np.zeros(6)
2. print(zeros_array)
```

Output:

```
[0. 0. 0. 0. 0. 0.]
```

You can create a 2-dimensional array of all zeros by passing the number of rows and columns as the first and second parameters of the **zeros()** method as shown below:

Script 8:

```
1. zeros_array = np.zeros((6,4))
2. print(zeros_array)
```

Output:

```
[[0. 0. 0. 0.]
 [0. 0. 0. 0.]
 [0. 0. 0. 0.]
 [0. 0. 0. 0.]
 [0. 0. 0. 0.]
 [0. 0. 0. 0.]]
```

3.2.5. Using Eyes Method

The **eye()** method is used to create an identity matrix in the form of a 2-dimensional NumPy array. An identity contains 1s along the diagonal, while the rest of the elements are 0 in the array.

Script 9:

```
1. eyes_array = np.eye(5)
2. print(eyes_array)
```

Output:

```
[[1. 0. 0. 0. 0.]
 [0. 1. 0. 0. 0.]
 [0. 0. 1. 0. 0.]
 [0. 0. 0. 1. 0.]
 [0. 0. 0. 0. 1.]]
```

3.2.6. Using Random Method

The **random.rand()** function from the NumPy module can be used to create a NumPy array with uniform distribution.

Script 10:

```
1.  uniform_random = np.random.rand(4, 5)
2.  print(uniform_random)
```

Output:

```
[[0.36728531 0.25376281 0.05039624 0.96432236 0.08579293]
 [0.29194804 0.93016399 0.88781312 0.50209692 0.63069239]
 [0.99952044 0.44384871 0.46041845 0.10246553 0.53461098]
 [0.75817916 0.36505441 0.01683344 0.9887365  0.21490949]]
```

The **random.randn()** function from the NumPy module can be used to create a NumPy array with normal distribution, as shown in the following example.

Script 11:

```
1.  normal_random = np.random.randn(4, 5)
2.  print(uniform_random)
```

Output:

```
[[0.36728531 0.25376281 0.05039624 0.96432236 0.08579293]
 [0.29194804 0.93016399 0.88781312 0.50209692 0.63069239]
 [0.99952044 0.44384871 0.46041845 0.10246553 0.53461098]
 [0.75817916 0.36505441 0.01683344 0.9887365  0.21490949]]
```

Finally, the **random.randint()** function from the NumPy module can be used to create a NumPy array with random integers between a certain range. The first parameter to the **randint()** function specifies the lower bound, the second parameter specifies the upper bound, while the last parameter specifies the number of random integers to generate between the range. The following example generates five random integers between 5 and 50.

Script 12:

```
1.  integer_random = np.random.randint(10, 50, 5)
2.  print(integer_random)
```

Output:

```
[25 49 21 35 17]
```

3.3. Reshaping NumPy Arrays

A NumPy array can be reshaped using the **reshape()** function. It is important to mention that the product of the rows and columns in the reshaped array must be equal to the product of rows and columns in the original array. For instance, in the following example, the original array contains four rows and six columns, i.e., 4 x 6 = 24. The reshaped array contains three rows and eight columns, i.e., 3 x 8 = 24.

Script 13:

```
1.  uniform_random = np.random.rand(4, 6)
2.  uniform_random = uniform_random.reshape(3, 8)
3.  print(uniform_random)
```

Output:

```
[[0.37576967 0.5425328  0.56087883 0.35265748 0.19677258
0.65107479  0.63287089  0.70649913]
 [0.47830882 0.3570451  0.82151482 0.09622735 0.1269332
0.65866216  0.31875221  0.91781242]
 [0.89785438 0.47306848 0.58350797 0.4604004  0.62352155
0.88064432  0.0859386  0.51918485]]
```

3.4. Array Indexing and Slicing

NumPy arrays can be indexed and sliced. Slicing an array means dividing an array into multiple parts.

NumPy arrays are indexed just like normal lists. Indexes in NumPy arrays start from 0, which means that the first item of a NumPy array is stored at the 0th index.

The following script creates a simple NumPy array of the first 10 positive integers.

Script 14:

```
1. s = np.arange(1,11)
2. print(s)
```

Output:

```
[ 1  2  3  4  5  6  7  8  9 10]
```

The item at index one can be accessed as follows:

Script 15:

```
print(s[1])
```

Output:

```
2
```

To slice an array, you have to pass the lower index, followed by a colon and the upper index. The items from the lower index (inclusive) to the upper index (exclusive) will be filtered. The following script slices the array "s" from the 1st index to the 9th index. The elements from index 1 to 8 are printed in the output.

Script 16:

```
print(s[1:9])
```

Output:

```
[2 3 4 5 6 7 8 9]
```

If you specify only the upper bound, all the items from the first index to the upper bound are returned. Similarly, if you specify only the lower bound, all the items from the lower bound to the last item of the array are returned.

Script 17:

```
1.  print(s[:5])
2.  print(s[5:])
```

Output:

```
[1 2 3 4 5]
[ 6  7  8  9 10]
```

Array slicing can also be applied on a 2-dimensional array. To do so, you have to apply slicing on arrays and columns separately. A comma separates the rows and columns slicing. In the following script, the rows from the first and second index are returned, While all the columns returned. You can see the first two complete rows in the output.

Script 18:

```
1.  row1 = [10,12,13]
2.  row2 = [45,32,16]
3.  row3 = [45,32,16]
4.
5.  nums_2d = np.array([row1, row2, row3])
6.  print(nums_2d[:2,:])
```

Output:

```
[[10 12 13]
 [45 32 16]]
```

Similarly, the following script returns all the rows but only the first two columns.

Script 19:

```
1.  row1 = [10,12,13]
2.  row2 = [45,32,16]
3.  row3 = [45,32,16]
4.
5.  nums_2d = np.array([row1, row2, row3])
6.  print(nums_2d[:,:2])
```

Output:

```
[[10 12]
 [45 32]
 [45 32]]
```

Let's see another example of slicing. Here, we will slice the rows from row one to the end of rows and column one to the end of columns. (Remember, row and column numbers start from 0.) In the output, you will see the last two rows and the last two columns.

Script 20:

```
1.  row1 = [10,12,13]
2.  row2 = [45,32,16]
3.  row3 = [45,32,16]
4.
5.  nums_2d = np.array([row1, row2, row3])
6.  print(nums_2d[1:,1:])
```

Output:

```
[[32 16]
 [32 16]]
```

3.5. NumPy for Arithmetic Operations

NumPy arrays provide a variety of functions to perform arithmetic operations. Some of these functions are explained in this section.

3.5.1. Finding Square Roots

The **sqrt()** function is used to find the square roots of all the elements in a list as shown below:

Script 21:

```
1.  nums = [10,20,30,40,50]
2.  np_sqr = np.sqrt(nums)
3.  print(np_sqr)
```

Output:

```
[3.16227766 4.47213595 5.47722558 6.32455532 7.07106781]
```

3.5.2. Finding Logs

The **log()** function is used to find the logs of all the elements in a list as shown below:

Script 22:

```
1.  nums = [10,20,30,40,50]
2.  np_log = np.log(nums)
3.  print(np_log )
```

Output:

```
[2.30258509 2.99573227 3.40119738 3.68887945 3.91202301]
```

3.5.3. Finding Exponents

The **exp()** function takes the exponents of all the elements in a list as shown below:

Script 23:

```
1.  nums = [10,20,30,40,50]
2.  np_exp = np.exp(nums)
3.  print(np_exp)
```

Output:

```
[2.20264658e+04 4.85165195e+08 1.06864746e+13 2.35385267e+17
 5.18470553e+21]
```

3.5.4. Finding Sine and Cosine

You can find the sines and cosines of items in a list using the sine and cosine function, respectively, as shown in the following script.

Script 24:

```
1.  nums = [10,20,30,40,50]
2.  np_sine = np.sin(nums)
3.  print(np_sine)
4.
5.  nums = [10,20,30,40,50]
6.  np_cos = np.cos(nums)
7.  print(np_cos)
```

Output:

```
[-0.54402111  0.91294525 -0.98803162  0.74511316 -0.26237485]
[-0.83907153  0.40808206  0.15425145 -0.66693806  0.96496603]
```

3.6. NumPy for Linear Algebra Operations

Data science makes extensive use of linear algebra. The support for performing advanced linear algebra functions in a fast and efficient way makes NumPy one of the most routinely used libraries for data science. In this section, you will perform some of the most linear algebraic operations with NumPy.

3.6.1. Finding Matrix Dot Product

To find a matrix dot product, you can use the **dot()** function. To find the dot product, the number of columns in the first matrix must match the number of rows in the second matrix. Here is an example.

Script 25:

```
1.  A = np.random.randn(4,5)
2.
3.  B = np.random.randn(5,4)
4.
5.  Z =  np.dot(A,B)
6.
7.  print(Z)
```

Output:

```
[[ 1.43837722 -4.74991285  1.42127048 -0.41569506]
 [-1.64613809  5.79380984 -1.33542482  1.53201023]
 [-1.31518878  0.72397674 -2.01300047  0.61651047]
 [-1.36765444  3.83694475 -0.56382045  0.21757162]]
```

3.6.2. Element-wise Matrix Multiplication

In addition to finding the dot product of two matrices, you can element-wise multiply two matrices. To do so, you can use the **multiply()** function. The dimensions of the two matrices must match.

Script 26:

```
1.  row1 = [10,12,13]
2.  row2 = [45,32,16]
3.  row3 = [45,32,16]
4.
5.  nums_2d = np.array([row1, row2, row3])
6.  multiply = np.multiply(nums_2d, nums_2d)
7.  print(multiply)
```

Output:

```
[[ 100  144  169]
 [2025 1024  256]
 [2025 1024  256]]
```

3.6.3. Finding Matrix Inverse

You find the inverse of a matrix via the **linalg.inv()** function as shown below:

Script 27:

```
1.  row1 = [1,2,3]
2.  row2 = [4,5,6]
3.  row3 = [7,8,9]
4.
5.  nums_2d = np.array([row1, row2, row3])
6.
7.  inverse = np.linalg.inv(nums_2d)
8.  print(inverse)
```

Output:

```
[[  3.15251974e+15  -6.30503948e+15   3.15251974e+15]
 [-6.30503948e+15   1.26100790e+16  -6.30503948e+15]
 [  3.15251974e+15  -6.30503948e+15   3.15251974e+15]]
```

3.6.4. Finding Matrix Determinant

Similarly, the determinant of a matrix can be found using the **linalg.det()** function as shown below:

Script 28:

```
1.  row1 = [1,2,3]
2.  row2 = [4,5,6]
3.  row3 = [7,8,9]
4.
5.  nums_2d = np.array([row1, row2, row3])
6.
7.  determinant = np.linalg.det(nums_2d)
8.  print(determinant)
```

Output:

```
-9.51619735392994e-16
```

3.6.5. Finding Matrix Trace

The trace of a matrix refers to the sum of all the elements along the diagonal of a matrix. To find the trace of a matrix, you can use the **trace()** function, as shown below:

Script 29:

```
1.  row1 = [1,2,3]
2.  row2 = [4,5,6]
3.  row3 = [7,8,9]
4.
5.  nums_2d = np.array([row1, row2, row3])
6.
7.  trace = np.trace(nums_2d)
8.  print(trace)
```

Output:

```
15
```

Exercise 3.1

Question 1:

Which NumPy function is used for the element-wise multiplication of two matrices?

    A. np.dot(matrix1, matrix2)

    B. np.multiply(matrix1, matrix2)

    C. np.elementwise(matrix1, matrix2)

    D. None of the above

Question 2:

To generate an identity matrix of four rows and four columns, which of the following functions can be used?

    A. np.identity(4,4)

    B. np.id(4,4)

    C. np.eye(4,4)

    D. All of the above

Question 3:

How to create the array of numbers 4,7,10,13,16 with NumPy:

    A. np.arange(3, 16, 3)

    B. np.arange(4, 16, 3)

    C. np.arange(4, 15,3)

    D. None of the above

Exercise 3.2

Create a random NumPy array of five rows and four columns. Using array indexing and slicing, display the items from row three to end and column two to end.

Introduction to Pandas Library for Data Analysis

4.1. Introduction

In this chapter, you will see how to use Python's Pandas library for data analysis. In the next chapter, you will see how to use the Pandas library for data visualization by plotting different types of plots.

Execute the following script on your command prompt to download the Pandas library.

```
$ pip install pandas
```

The following script imports the Pandas library in your application. Execute the script at the type of all Python codes that are provided in this chapter.

```
import pandas as pd
```

Furthermore, the following are the libraries that you need to install before running scripts in this chapter.

4.2. Reading Data into Pandas Dataframe

In the second chapter of this book, you saw how the Pandas library can be used to read CSV and TSV files. Here, we will briefly recap how to read a CSV file with Pandas. The following script reads the "titanic_data.csv" file from the *Datasets* folder in the GitHub repository. The first five rows of the Titanic dataset have been printed via the **head()** method of the Pandas dataframe containing the Titanic dataset.

Script 1:

```
1. import pandas as pd
2. titanic_data = pd.read_csv(r"E:\
   Data Visualization with Python\Datasets\titanic_data.csv")
3. titanic_data.head()
```

Output:

PassengerId	Survived	Pclass	Name	Sex	Age	SibSp	Parch	Ticket	Fare	Cabin	Embarked
0	1	0	3	Braund, Mr. Owen Harris	male	22.0	1	0	A/5 21171	7.2500	NaN	S
1	2	1	1	Cumings, Mrs. John Bradley (Florence Briggs Th...	female	38.0	1	0	PC 17599	71.2833	C85	C
2	3	1	3	Heikkinen, Miss. Laina	female	26.0	0	0	STON/O2. 3101282	7.9250	NaN	S
3	4	1	1	Futrelle, Mrs. Jacques Heath (Lily May Peel)	female	35.0	1	0	113803	53.1000	C123	S
4	5	0	3	Allen, Mr. William Henry	male	35.0	0	0	373450	8.0500	NaN	S

The **read_csv()** method reads data from a CSV or TSV file and stores it in a Pandas dataframe, which is a special object that stores data in the form of rows and columns.

4.3. Filtering Rows

One of the most routine tasks that you need to perform while handling Pandas dataframe is to filter rows based on column values.

To filter rows, you have to first identify the indexes of the rows to filter. For those indexes, you need to pass True to the opening and closing square brackets that follow the Pandas dataframe name.

The following script returns a series of True and False. True will be returned for indexes where the Pclass column has a value of 1.

Script 2:

```
1.  titanic_pclass1= (titanic_data.Pclass == 1)
2.  titanic_pclass1
```

Output:

```
0        False
1         True
2        False
3         True
4        False
         ...
886      False
887       True
888      False
889       True
890      False
Name: Pclass, Length: 891, dtype: bool
```

Now, the **titanic_pclass1** series, which contains True or False, can be passed inside the opening and closing square brackets that follow the **titanic_data** dataframe. The result will be a Titanic dataset containing only those records where the Pclass column contains 1.

Script 3:

```
1.  titanic_pclass1= (titanic_data.Pclass == 1)
2.  titanic_pclass1_data = titanic_data[titanic_pclass1]
3.  titanic_pclass1_data.head()
```

Output:

	PassengerId	Survived	Pclass	Name	Sex	Age	SibSp	Parch	Ticket	Fare	Cabin	Embarked
1	2	1	1	Cumings, Mrs. John Bradley (Florence Briggs Th...	male	38.0	1	0	PC 17599	71.2833	C85	C
3	4	1	1	Futrelle, Mrs. Jacques Heath (Lily May Peel)	male	35.0	1	0	113803	53.1000	C123	S
6	7	0	1	McCarthy, Mr. Timothy J	male	54.0	0	0	17463	51.8625	E46	S
11	12	1	1	Bonnell, Miss. Elizabeth	male	58.0	0	0	113783	26.5500	C103	S
23	24	1	1	Sloper, Mr. William Thompson	male	28.0	0	0	113788	35.5000	A6	S

The comparison between the column values and filtering of rows can be done in a single line as shown below:

Script 4:

```
1. titanic_pclass_data = titanic_data[titanic_data.
   Pclass == 1]
2. titanic_pclass_data.head()
```

Output:

PassengerId	Survived	Pclass	Name	Sex	Age	SibSp	Parch	Ticket	Fare	Cabin	Embarked
1	2	1	1	Cumings, Mrs. John Bradley (Florence Briggs Th...	male	38.0	1	0	PC 17599	71.2833	C85	C
3	4	1	1	Futrelle, Mrs Jacques Heath (Lily May Peel)	male	35.0	1	0	113803	53.1000	C123	S
6	7	0	1	McCarthy, Mr. Timothy J	male	54.0	0	0	17463	51.8625	E46	S
11	12	1	1	Bonnell, Miss. Elizabeth	male	58.0	0	0	113783	26.5500	C103	S
23	24	1	1	Sloper, Mr. William Thompson	male	28.0	0	0	113788	35.5000	A6	S

Another commonly used operator to filter rows is the **isin** operator. The **isin** operator takes a list of values and returns only those rows where the column used for comparison contains values from the list passed to the **isin** operator as a parameter. For instance, the following script filters those rows where age is 20, 21, or 22.

Script 5:

```
1. ages = [20,21,22]
2. age_dataset = titanic_data[titanic_data["Age"].isin(ages)]
3. age_dataset.head()
```

Output:

PassengerId	Survived	Pclass	Name	Sex	Age	SibSp	Parch	Ticket	Fare	Cabin	Embarked
0	1	0	3	Braund, Mr. Owen Harris	male	22.0	1	0	A/5 21171	7.25	NaN	S
12	13	0	3	Saundercock, Mr. William Henry	male	20.0	0	0	A/5. 2151	8.05	NaN	S
37	38	0	3	Cann, Mr. Ernest Charles	male	21.0	0	0	A./5. 2152	8.05	NaN	S
51	52	0	3	Nosworthy, Mr. Richard Cater	male	21.0	0	0	A/4. 39886	7.80	NaN	S
56	57	1	2	Rugg, Miss. Emily	male	21.0	0	0	C.A. 31026	10.50	NaN	S

You can filter rows in a Pandas dataframe based on multiple conditions using logical and (&) and or (|) operators. The following script returns those rows from the Pandas dataframe where passenger class is 1 and passenger age is 20, 21, and 22.

Script 6:

```
1. ages = [20,21,22]
2. ageclass_dataset = titanic_data[titanic_data["Age"].
   isin(ages) & (titanic_data["Pclass"] == 1) ]
3. ageclass_dataset.head()
```

Output:

	PassengerId	Survived	Pclass	Name	Sex	Age	SibSp	Parch	Ticket	Fare	Cabin	Embarked
102	103	0	1	White, Mr. Richard Frasar	male	21.0	0	1	35281	77.2875	D26	S
151	152	1	1	Pears, Mrs. Thomas (Edith Wearne)	male	22.0	1	0	113776	66.6000	C2	S
356	357	1	1	Bowerman, Miss. Elsie Edith	male	22.0	0	1	113505	55.0000	E33	S
373	374	0	1	Ringhini, Mr. Sante	male	22.0	0	0	PC 17760	135.6333	NaN	C
539	540	1	1	Frolicher, Miss. Hedwig Margaritha	male	22.0	0	2	13568	49.5000	B39	C

4.4. Filtering Columns

To filter columns from a Pandas dataframe, you can use the **filter()** method. The list of columns that you want to filter is passed to the filter() method. The following script filters Name, Sex, and Age columns from the Titanic dataset and ignores all the other columns.

Script 7:

```
1. titanic_data_filter  = titanic_data.
   filter(["Name", "Sex", "Age"])
2. titanic_data_filter.head()
```

The output below shows that the dataset now contains only Name, Sex, and Age columns.

Output:

	Name	Sex	Age
0	Braund, Mr. Owen Harris	male	22.0
1	Cumings, Mrs. John Bradley (Florence Briggs Th...	female	38.0
2	Heikkinen, Miss. Laina	female	26.0
3	Futrelle, Mrs. Jacques Heath (Lily May Peel)	female	35.0
4	Allen, Mr. William Henry	male	35.0

In addition to filtering columns, you can also drop columns that you don't want in the dataset. To do so, you need to call the **drop()** method and pass it the list of columns that you want to drop. For instance, the following script drops the Name, Age, and Sex columns from the Titanic dataset and returns the remaining columns.

Script 8:

```
1. titanic_data_filter = titanic_data.
   drop(["Name", "Sex", "Age"], axis = 1)
2. itanic_data_filter.head()
```

Output:

	PassengerId	Survived	Pclass	SibSp	Parch	Ticket	Fare	Cabin	Embarked
0	1	0	3	1	0	A/5 21171	7.2500	NaN	S
1	2	1	1	1	0	PC 17599	71.2833	C85	C
2	3	1	3	0	0	STON/O2. 3101282	7.9250	NaN	S
3	4	1	1	1	0	113803	53.1000	C123	S
4	5	0	3	0	0	373450	8.0500	NaN	S

Further Readings – Pandas Filter

To study more about the Pandas Filter method, please check Pandas' official documentation for the filter method (https://bit.ly/2C8SWhB). Try to execute the filter method with a different set of attributes, as mentioned in the official documentation.

4.5. Concatenating Dataframes

Oftentimes, you need to concatenate or join multiple Pandas dataframes horizontally or vertically. Let's first see how to concatenate or join Pandas dataframes vertically. We will first create two Pandas dataframes using Titanic data. The first dataframe contains rows where the passenger class is 1, while the second dataframe contains rows where the passenger class is 2.

Script 9:

```
1. titanic_pclass1_data = titanic_data[titanic_data.
   Pclass == 1]
2. print(titanic_pclass1_data.shape)
3.
4. titanic_pclass2_data = titanic_data[titanic_data.
   Pclass == 2]
5. print(titanic_pclass2_data.shape)
```

Output:

(216, 12)
(184, 12)

The output shows that both the newly created dataframes have 12 columns. It is important to mention that while concatenating data vertically, both the dataframes should have an equal number of columns.

There are two ways to concatenate datasets horizontally. You can call the **append()** method via the first dataframe and pass the second dataframe as a parameter to the **append()** method. Look at the following script:

Script 10:

```
1. final_data = titanic_pclass1_data.append(titanic_pclass2_
   data, ignore_index=True)
2. print(final_data.shape)
```

Output:

(400, 12)

The output now shows that the total number of rows is 400, which is the sum of the number of rows in the two dataframes that we concatenated.

Further Readings – Pandas append

To study more about the Pandas append method, please check Pandas' official documentation for the append method (https://bit.ly/2CaSteR). Try to execute the append method with a different set of attributes, as mentioned in the official documentation.

The other way to concatenate two dataframes is by passing both the dataframes as parameters to the **concat()** method of the Pandas module. The following script shows how to do that.

Script 11:

```
1. final_data = pd.concat([titanic_pclass1_data, titanic_
   pclass2_data])
2. print(final_data.shape)
```

Output:

(400, 12)

To concatenate dataframes horizontally, make sure that the dataframes have an equal number of rows. You can use the **concat()** method to concatenate dataframes horizontally as well. However, you will need to pass 1 as the value for the **axis** attribute. Furthermore, to reset dataset indexes, you need to pass True as the value for the **ignore_index** attribute.

Script 12:

```
1. df1 = final_data[:200]
2. print(df1.shape)
3. df2 = final_data[200:]
4. print(df2.shape)
5.
6. final_data2 = pd.concat([df1, df2], axis = 1, ignore_
   index = True)
7. print(final_data2.shape)
```

Output:

```
(200, 12)
(200, 12)
(400, 24)
```

Further Readings – Pandas concat

To study more about the Pandas concat() method, please check Pandas' official documentation for the concat method (https://bit.ly/2PDnDyJ). Try to execute the concat method with a different set of attributes, as mentioned in the official documentation.

4.6. Sorting Dataframes

To sort the Pandas dataframe, you can use the **sort_values()** function of the Pandas dataframe. The list of columns used for sorting needs to be passed to the **by** attribute of the **sort_values()** method. The following script sorts the Titanic dataset in ascending order of the passenger's age.

Script 13:

```
1. age_sorted_data = titanic_data.sort_values(by=['Age'])
2. age_sorted_data.head()
```

Output:

	PassengerId	Survived	Pclass	Name	Sex	Age	SibSp	Parch	Ticket	Fare	Cabin	Embarked
803	804	1	3	Thomas, Master. Assad Alexander	male	0.42	0	1	2625	8.5167	NaN	C
755	756	1	2	Hamalainen, Master. Viljo	male	0.67	1	1	250649	14.5000	NaN	S
644	645	1	3	Baclini, Miss. Eugenie	male	0.75	2	1	2666	19.2583	NaN	C
469	470	1	3	Baclini, Miss. Helene Barbara	male	0.75	2	1	2666	19.2583	NaN	C
78	79	1	2	Caldwell, Master. Alden Gates	male	0.83	0	2	248738	29.0000	NaN	S

To sort by descending order, you need to pass False as the value for the **ascending** attribute of the **sort_values()** function. The following script sorts the dataset by descending order of age.

Script 14:

```
1.  age_sorted_data = titanic_data.sort_
    values(by=['Age'], ascending = False)
2.  age_sorted_data.head()
```

Output:

	PassengerId	Survived	Pclass	Name	Sex	Age	SibSp	Parch	Ticket	Fare	Cabin	Embarked
630	631	1	1	Barkworth, Mr. Algernon Henry Wilson	male	80.0	0	0	27042	30.0000	A23	S
851	852	0	3	Svensson, Mr. Johan	male	74.0	0	0	347060	7.7750	NaN	S
493	494	0	1	Artagaveytia, Mr. Ramon	male	71.0	0	0	PC 17609	49.5042	NaN	C
96	97	0	1	Goldschmidt, Mr. George B	male	71.0	0	0	PC 17754	34.6542	A5	C
116	117	0	3	Connors, Mr. Patrick	male	70.5	0	0	370369	7.7500	NaN	Q

You can also pass multiple columns to the **by** attribute of the **sort_values()** function. In such a case, the dataset will be sorted by the first column, and in case of equal values for two or more records, the dataset will be sorted by the second column and so on. The following script first sorts the data by Age and then by Fare, both by descending orders.

Script 15:

```
1.  age_sorted_data = titanic_data.sort_
    values(by=['Age','Fare'], ascending = False)
2.  age_sorted_data.head()
```

Output:

	PassengerId	Survived	Pclass	Name	Sex	Age	SibSp	Parch	Ticket	Fare	Cabin	Embarked
630	631	1	1	Barkworth, Mr. Algernon Henry Wilson	male	80.0	0	0	27042	30.0000	A23	S
851	852	0	3	Svensson, Mr. Johan	male	74.0	0	0	347060	7.7750	NaN	S
493	494	0	1	Artagaveytia, Mr. Ramon	male	71.0	0	0	PC 17609	49.5042	NaN	C
96	97	0	1	Goldschmidt, Mr. George B	male	71.0	0	0	PC 17754	34.6542	A5	C
116	117	0	3	Connors, Mr. Patrick	male	70.5	0	0	370369	7.7500	NaN	Q

Further Readings – Pandas sort_values

To study more about Pandas sort_values() method, please check Pandas' official documentation for sort_values() method (https://bit.ly/2PD41dU). Try to execute the sort_values() method with a different set of attributes, as mentioned in the official documentation.

4.7. Apply Function

The **apply()** function is used to apply a function on multiple rows or on rows of a particular column. A lambda expression is passed to the **apply()** function. The lambda expression basically specifies the operation performed by the **apply()** function. For instance, in the following, the **apply()** function adds 2 to all the values in the **Pclass** column of the Titanic dataset.

Script 16:

```
1. updated_class = titanic_data.Pclass.apply(lambda x : x + 2)
2. pdated_class.head()
```

The output shows that all the values in the Pclass column have been incremented by 2.

Output:
```
0    5
1    3
```

2   5
3   3
4   5

Name: Pclass, dtype: int64

In addition to a lambda expression, you can also pass a concrete function to the **apply()** method. In the following script, we define a **mult()** function, which multiplies the parameter passed to it by 2 and returns the resultant value. In the apply function, we simply pass the name of the **mult()** method. All the values in the **Pclass** column will be multiplied by 2, as shown in the output of the script 17.

Script 17:

```
1. def mult(x):
2.     return x * 2
3.
4. updated_class = titanic_data.Pclass.apply(mult)
5. updated_class.head()
```

Output:

0   6
1   2
2   6
3   2
4   6

Name: Pclass, dtype: int64

Further Readings – Pandas apply

To study more about the Pandas apply method, please check Pandas' official documentation for the apply method (https://bit.ly/3kxvBb1). Try to execute the apply method with a different set of attributes, as mentioned in the official documentation.

4.8. Pivot & Crosstab

You have already seen the Pivot operator in action in the last chapter when we studied heat maps in Seaborn. Here, we will briefly revise the pivot operation via the Flights dataset. The following script downloads the Flights dataset.

Script 18:

```
1. import matplotlib.pyplot as plt
2. import seaborn as sns
3.
4.
5. flights_data = sns.load_dataset('flights')
6.
7. flights_data.head()
```

Output:

	year	month	passengers
0	1949	January	112
1	1949	February	118
2	1949	March	132
3	1949	April	129
4	1949	May	121

Script 19:

```
1. flights_data_pivot =flights_data.pivot_table(index=
   'month', columns='year', values='passengers')
2. flights_data_pivot.head()
```

Output:

year	1949	1950	1951	1952	1953	1954	1955	1956	1957	1958	1959	1960
month												
January	112	115	145	171	196	204	242	284	315	340	360	417
February	118	126	150	180	196	188	233	277	301	318	342	391
March	132	141	178	193	236	235	267	317	356	362	406	419
April	129	135	163	181	235	227	269	313	348	348	396	461
May	121	125	172	183	229	234	270	318	355	363	420	472

The **crosstab()** function is used to plot cross tabulation between two columns. Let's plot a cross tab matrix between passenger class and age columns for the Titanic dataset.

Script 20:

```
1. import pandas as pd
2. titanic_data = pd.read_csv(r"E:\
   Data Visualization with Python\Datasets\titanic_data.csv")
3. titanic_data.head()
4.
5. pd.crosstab(titanic_data.Pclass, titanic_data.
   Age, margins=True)
```

Output:

Age	0.42	0.67	0.75	0.83	0.92	1.0	2.0	3.0	4.0	5.0	...	63.0	64.0	65.0	66.0	70.0	70.5	71.0	74.0	80.0	All
Pclass																					
1	0	0	0	0	1	0	1	0	1	0	...	1	2	2	0	1	0	2	0	1	186
2	0	1	0	2	0	2	2	3	2	1	...	0	0	0	1	1	0	0	0	0	173
3	1	0	2	0	0	5	7	3	7	3	...	1	0	1	0	0	1	0	1	0	355
All	1	1	2	2	1	7	10	6	10	4	...	2	2	3	1	2	1	2	1	1	714

4 rows × 89 columns

4.9. Arithmetic Operations with Where

The **where** clause from the **numpy** library can be used to perform arithmetic operations on Pandas dataframe. For instance, in the following script, the **where** clause is used to add 5 to the rows in the Fare column, **where** passengers' ages are greater than 20.

Script 21:

```
1. import numpy as np
2. titanic_data.Fare = np.where( titanic_data.
   Age > 20, titanic_data.Fare +5 , titanic_data.Fare)
3.
4. titanic_data.head()
```

Output:

	PassengerId	Survived	Pclass	Name	Sex	Age	SibSp	Parch	Ticket	Fare	Cabin	Embarked
0	1	0	3	Braund, Mr. Owen Harris	male	22.0	1	0	A/5 21171	17.2500	NaN	S
1	2	1	1	Cumings, Mrs. John Bradley (Florence Briggs Th...	female	38.0	1	0	PC 17599	81.2833	C85	C
2	3	1	3	Heikkinen, Miss. Laina	female	26.0	0	0	STON/O2. 3101282	17.9250	NaN	S
3	4	1	1	Futrelle, Mrs. Jacques Heath (Lily May Peel)	female	35.0	1	0	113803	63.1000	C123	S
4	5	0	3	Allen, Mr. William Henry	male	35.0	0	0	373450	18.0500	NaN	S

Hands-on Time – Exercise

Now, it is your turn. Follow the instructions in **the exercises below** to check your understanding of data analysis with the Pandas library. The answers to these exercises are provided after chapter 10 in this book.

Exercise 4.1

Question 1

In order to horizontally concatenate two Pandas dataframes, the value for the axis attribute should be set to:

    A. 0

    B. 1

    C. 2

    D. None of the above

Question 2

Which function is used to sort a Pandas dataframe by column value?

    A. sort_dataframe()

    B. sort_rows()

    C. sort_values()

    D. sort_records()

Question 3

To filter columns from a Pandas dataframe, you have to pass a list of column names to one of the following methods:

    A. filter()

    B. filter_columns()

    C. apply_filter()

    D. None of the above()

Exercise 4.2

Use the apply function to subtract 10 from the Fare column of the Titanic dataset, without using a lambda expression.

Data Visualization via Matplotlib, Seaborn, and Pandas Libraries

5.1. What is Data Visualization?

Data visualization is the process of visualizing data in order to identify important patterns in the data that can be used for organizational decision making. Visualizing data graphically can reveal trends that otherwise may remain hidden from the naked eye.

Data visualization is a precursor to many important processes such as Data Science, Machine Learning, Business Intelligence, and Data Analytics. Data visualization is, doubtless, one of the most important skillsets of the 21st century for a variety of jobs.

In this chapter, you will see some of the most commonly used Python libraries for data visualization. You will see how to plot different types of plots using Maplotlib, Seaborn, and Pandas libraries.

5.2. Data Visualization via Matplotlib

In this section, we will start a formal discussion about Matplotlib, which is one of the most commonly and frequently used Python libraries for data visualization. Matplotlib is so popular that various advanced data visualization libraries such as Seaborn use Matplotlib as the underlying data visualization library.

Finally, before you can plot any graphs with Matplotlib library, you will need to import the **pyplot** module from the Matplotlib library. And since all the scripts will be executed inside Jupyter Notebook, the statement **%matplotlib inline** has been used to generate plots inside Jupyter Notebook. Execute the following script:

```
1. import matplotlib.pyplot as plt
2. %matplotlib inline
```

5.2.1. Line Plots

A line plot is the first plot that we are going to plot in this chapter. A line plot is the easiest of all the Matplotlib plots. This plot is basically used to plot the relationship between two numerical sets of values. Usually, a line plot is used to plot an increasing or decreasing trend between two dependent variables. For instance, if you want to see how the weather changed over a period of 24 hours, you can use a line plot, where the x-axis contains hourly information, and the y-axis contains weather in degrees. Let us plot a line plot that displays the square root of 20 equidistance numbers between 0 and 20. Look at Script 1:

Script 1:

```
1.  import matplotlib.pyplot as plt
2.  import numpy as np
3.  import math
4.
5.  x_vals = np.linspace(0, 20, 20)
6.  y_vals = [math.sqrt(i) for i in x_vals]
7.  plt.plot(x_vals, y_vals)
```

In script 1, we generate 20 equidistant numbers using **np.linspace()** function. The numbers are stored in the **x_vals** variable. Next, we iterate through each value in the **x_vals** list and take the square root of each value. The resultant list is stored in the **y_vals** variable. To plot a line plot via the **pyplot** module, you only need to call the **plot()** method of the **pyplot** module and then pass it the values for the x and y axes. It is important to mention that **plt** is an alias for **pyplot** in script 1, and you can name it anything you want. Here is the output for script 1.

Output:

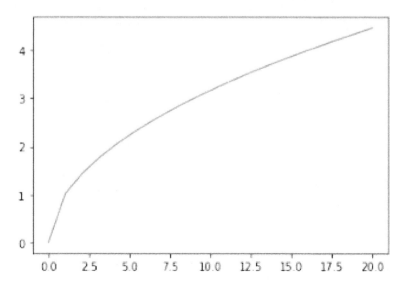

This is one of the ways to plot a graph via Matplotlib. There is also another way to do this. You first have to call the **figure()** method via the **plt** module, which draws an empty figure. Next, you can call the **axes()** method, which returns an **axes** object. You can then call the **plot()** method from the **axes** object to create a plot, as shown in the following script.

Script 2:

```
1.  import matplotlib.pyplot as plt
2.  import numpy as np
3.  import math
4.
5.  x_vals = np.linspace(0, 20, 20)
6.  y_vals = [math.sqrt(i) for i in x_vals]
7.
8.  fig = plt.figure()
9.  ax = plt.axes()
10. ax.plot(x_vals, y_vals)
```

Here is the output of the above script. This method can be used to plot multiple plots, which we will see in the next chapter. In this chapter, we will stick to the first approach, where we call the **plot()** method directly from the **pyplot** module.

Output:

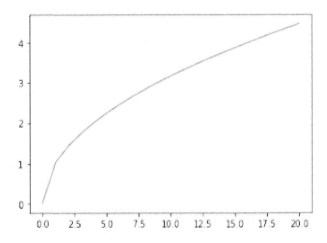

You can also increase the default plot size of a Matplotlib plot. To do so, you can use the **rcParams** list of the **pyplot** module and then set two values for the **figure.figsize** attribute. The following script sets the plot size to 8 inches wide and 6 inches tall.

Script 3:

```
1.  import matplotlib.pyplot as plt
2.  import numpy as np
3.  import math
4.
5.  plt.rcParams["figure.figsize"] = [8,6]
6.
7.  x_vals = np.linspace(0, 20, 20)
8.  y_vals = [math.sqrt(i) for i in x_vals]
9.  plt.plot(x_vals, y_vals)
```

In the output, you can see that the default plot size has been increased.

Output:

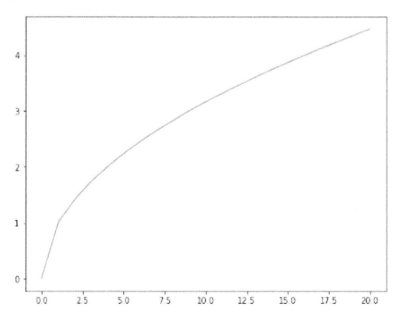

5.2.2. Titles, Labels, and Legends

You can improve the aesthetics and readability of your graphs by adding titles, labels, and legends to your graph. Let's first see how to add titles and labels to a plot.

To add labels on x and y axes, you need to pass the string values respectively to the **xlabel** and **ylabel** methods of the **pyplot** module. Similarly, to set the title, you need to pass a string value to the **title** method, as shown in script 4.

Script 4:

```
1.  import matplotlib.pyplot as plt
2.  import numpy as np
3.  import math
4.
5.  x_vals = np.linspace(0, 20, 20)
6.  y_vals = [math.sqrt(i) for i in x_vals]
7.  plt.xlabel('X Values')
8.  plt.ylabel('Y Values')
9.  plt.title('Square Roots')
10. plt.plot(x_vals, y_vals)
```

Here, in the output, you can see the labels and title that you specified in the script 4.

Output:

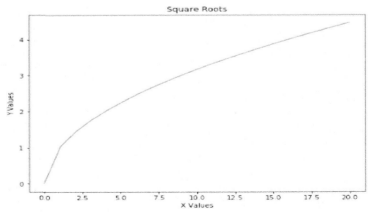

In addition to changing the titles and labels, you can also specify the color for the line plot. To do so, you simply have to pass shorthand notation for the color name to the **plot()** function, for example, "r" for red, "b" for blue, and so on. Here is an example:

Script 5:

```
1.  import matplotlib.pyplot as plt
2.  import numpy as np
3.  import math
4.
5.
6.  x_vals = np.linspace(0, 20, 20)
7.  y_vals = [math.sqrt(i) for i in x_vals]
8.  plt.xlabel('X Values')
9.  plt.ylabel('Y Values')
10. plt.title('Square Roots')
11. plt.plot(x_vals, y_vals, 'r')
```

Output:

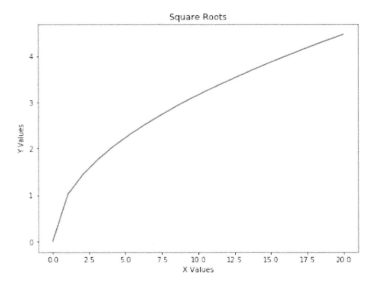

To add a legend, you need to make two changes. First, you have to pass a string value for the **label** attribute of the plot() function. Next, you have to pass the value for the **loc** attribute of the **legend** method of the **pyplot** module. In the **loc** attribute, you have to pass the location of your legend. The following script plots a legend at the upper center corner of the plot.

Script 6:

```
1.  import matplotlib.pyplot as plt
2.  import numpy as np
3.  import math
4.
5.
6.  x_vals = np.linspace(0, 20, 20)
7.  y_vals = [math.sqrt(i) for i in x_vals]
8.  plt.xlabel('X Values')
9.  plt.ylabel('Y Values')
10. plt.title('Square Roots')
11. plt.plot(x_vals, y_vals, 'r', label = 'Square Root')
12. plt.legend(loc='upper center')
```

Output:

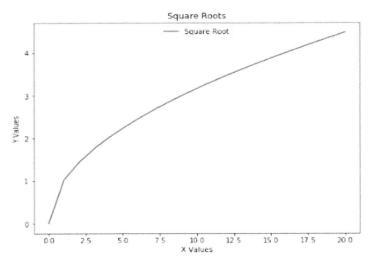

You can also plot multiple line plots inside one graph. All you have to do is call the **plot()** method twice with different values for x and y axes. The following script plots a line plot for square root in red and for a cube function in blue.

Script 7:

```
1.  import matplotlib.pyplot as plt
2.  import numpy as np
3.  import math
4.
5.
6.  x_vals = np.linspace(0, 20, 20)
7.  y_vals = [math.sqrt(i) for i in x_vals]
8.  y2_vals = x_vals ** 3
9.  plt.xlabel('X Values')
10. plt.ylabel('Y Values')
11. plt.title('Square Roots')
12. plt.plot(x_vals, y_vals, 'r', label = 'Square Root')
13. plt.plot(x_vals, y2_vals, 'b', label = 'Cube')
14. plt.legend(loc='upper center')
```

Output:

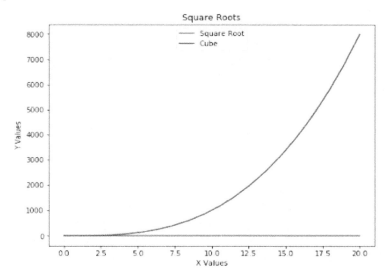

> **Further Readings – Matplotlib Line Plot**
>
> To study more about the Matplotlib line plot, please check Matplotlib's official documentation for line plots (https://bit.ly/33BqslR). Get used to searching and reading this documentation. It is a great resource of knowledge.

5.2.3. Plotting Using CSV and TSV files

In addition to plotting Matplotlib's graph using in-memory data, you can read data from sources such as CSV (Comma Separated View) and TSV (Tab Separated View) files. The best way to read data from a CSV file is via the **read_csv()** method of the Pandas library. You will study the Pandas library in detail in another chapter. For now, just keep in mind that the **read_csv()** method from the Pandas library can read CSV files and store the file data in a Pandas **dataframe**. Let's read the **iris_data.csv** file. The file is available in the *Datasets* folder in the GitHub repository. You can download locally. In the **read_csv()** method, you simply have to pass the path of the CSV file. An example is given in script 8.

Script 8:

```
1. import pandas as pd
2. data = pd.read_csv("E:\Data Visualization with Python\
   Datasets\iris_data.csv")
```

If you do not see any error, the file has been read successfully. To see the first five rows of the Pandas **dataframe** containing the data, you can use the **head()** method as shown below:

Script 9:

```
data.head()
```

Output:

	sepal_length	sepal_width	petal_length	petal_width	species
0	5.1	3.5	1.4	0.2	setosa
1	4.9	3.0	1.4	0.2	setosa
2	4.7	3.2	1.3	0.2	setosa
3	4.6	3.1	1.5	0.2	setosa
4	5.0	3.6	1.4	0.2	setosa

You can see that the **iris_data.csv** file has five columns. We can use values from any of these two columns to plot a line plot. To do so, for x and y axes, we need to pass the data **dataframe** column names to the **plot()** function of the **pyplot** module. To access a column name from a Pandas **dataframe**, you need to specify the **dataframe** name followed by a pair of square brackets. Inside the brackets, the column name is specified. The following script plots a line plot where the x-axis contains values from the **sepal_length** column, whereas the y-axis contains values from the **petal_length** column of the **dataframe**.

Script 10:

```
1. import matplotlib.pyplot as plt
2. import numpy as np
3. import math
4.
5. plt.xlabel('Sepal Length')
6. plt.ylabel('Petal Length')
7. plt.title('Sepal vs Petal Length')
8. plt.plot(data["sepal_length"], data["petal_length"], 'b')
```

Output:

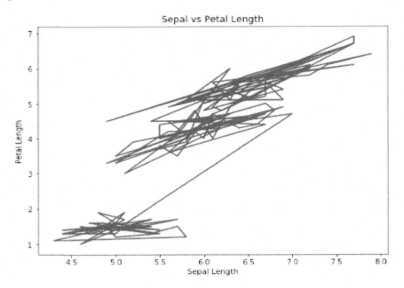

Like CSV, you can also read a TSV file via the **read_csv()** method. You have to pass **'\t'** as the value for the **sep** parameter. The script 11 reads **iris_data.tsv** file and stores it in a Pandas **dataframe.** Next, the first five rows of the dataframe have been printed via the **head()** method.

Script 11:

```
1.  import pandas as pd
2.  data = pd.read_csv("E:\Data Visualization with Python\
    Datasets\iris_data.tsv", sep='\t')
3.  data.head()
```

Output:

	SepalLength	SepalWidth	PetalLength	PetalWidth	TrainingClass
0	5.1	3.5	1.4	0.2	Iris-setosa
1	4.9	3.0	1.4	0.2	Iris-setosa
2	4.7	3.2	1.3	0.2	Iris-setosa
3	4.6	3.1	1.5	0.2	Iris-setosa
4	5.0	3.6	1.4	0.2	Iris-setosa

The remaining process to plot the line plot remains the same, as it was for the CSV file. The following script plots a line plot, where the x-axis contains sepal length, and the y-axis displays petal length.

Script 12:

```
1.  import matplotlib.pyplot as plt
2.  import numpy as np
3.  import math
4.
5.  plt.xlabel('Sepal Length')
6.  plt.ylabel('Petal Length')
7.  plt.title('Sepal vs Petal Length')
8.  plt.plot(data["SepalLength"], data["PetalLength"], "b")
```

Output:

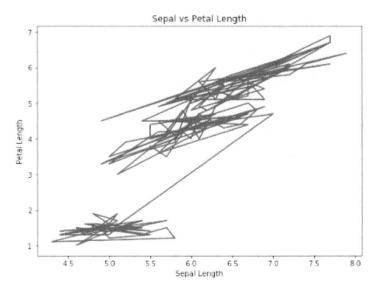

5.2.4. Scatter Plots

A Scatter plot is used essentially to plot the relationship between two numeric columns in the form of scattered points. Normally, a scattered plot is used when for each value in the x-axis, there exist multiple values in the y-axis. To plot a scatter plot, the **scatter()** function of the **pyplot** module is used. You have to pass the values for the x-axis and y-axis. In addition, you have to pass a shorthand notation of color value to the **c** parameter. Script 13 shows how to plot a scatter plot between sepal length and petal length of iris plants.

Script 13:

```
1.  import matplotlib.pyplot as plt
2.  import numpy as np
3.  import math
4.
5.  plt.xlabel('Sepal Length')
6.  plt.ylabel('Petal Length')
7.  plt.title('Sepal vs Petal Length')
8.  plt.
    scatter(data["SepalLength"], data["PetalLength"], c = "b")
```

The output shows a scattered plot with blue points. The plot clearly shows that with an increase in sepal length, the petal length of an iris flower also increases.

Output:

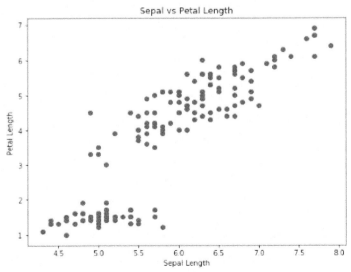

> **Further Readings – Matplotlib Scatter Plot**
>
> To study more about Matplotlib scatter plot, please check Matplotlib's official documentation for scatter plots (https://bit.ly/3a8Dtef). Get used to searching and reading this documentation. It is a great resource of knowledge.

5.2.5. Bar Plots

Bar plot is used to plot the relationship between unique values in a categorical column grouped by an aggregate function such as sum, mean, median, etc. Before we plot a bar plot, let's first import the dataset that we are going to use in this chapter. Execute the following script to read the **titanic_data. csv** file. You will find the CSV file in the Datasets folder in the GitHub repository. The following script also displays the first five rows of the dataset.

Script 14:

```
1. import pandas as pd
2. data = pd.read_csv(r"E:\Data Visualization with Python\
   Datasets\titanic_data.csv")
3. data.head()
```

Output:

PassengerId	Survived	Pclass	Name	Sex	Age	SibSp	Parch	Ticket	Fare	Cabin	Embarked
0	1	0	3	Braund, Mr. Owen Harris	male	22.0	1	0	A/5 21171	7.2500	NaN	S
1	2	1	1	Cumings, Mrs. John Bradley (Florence Briggs Th...	female	38.0	1	0	PC 17599	71.2833	C85	C
2	3	1	3	Heikkinen, Miss. Laina	female	26.0	0	0	STON/O2. 3101282	7.9250	NaN	S
3	4	1	1	Futrelle, Mrs. Jacques Heath (Lily May Peel)	female	35.0	1	0	113803	53.1000	C123	S
4	5	0	3	Allen, Mr. William Henry	male	35.0	0	0	373450	8.0500	NaN	S

To plot a bar plot, you need to call the **bar()** method. The categorical values are passed as the x-axis and corresponding aggregated numerical values are passed on the y-axis. The following script plots a bar plot between genders and ages of the passengers on the Titanic ship.

Script 15:

```
1.  import matplotlib.pyplot as plt
2.  import numpy as np
3.  import math
4.
5.  plt.xlabel('Gender')
6.  plt.ylabel('Ages')
7.  plt.title('Gender vs Age')
8.  plt.bar(data["Sex"], data["Age"])
```

Output:

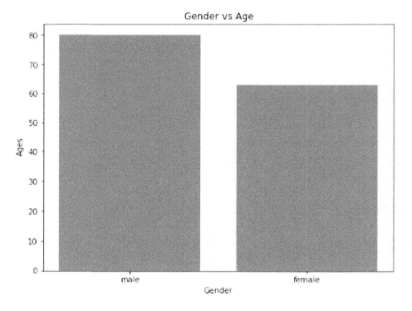

Further Readings – Matplotlib Bar Plot

To study more about Matplotlib bar plots, please check Matplotlib's official documentation for bar plots (https://bit.ly/2PNKR5r). Get used to searching and reading this documentation. It is a great resource of knowledge.

5.2.6. Histograms

Histograms are basically used to display the distribution of data for a numeric list of items. The **hist()** method is used to plot a histogram. You simply have to pass a collection of numeric values to the **hist()** method. For instance, the following histogram plots the distribution of values in the Age column of the Titanic dataset.

Script 16:

```
1.  import matplotlib.pyplot as plt
2.  import numpy as np
3.  import math
4.
5.  plt.title('Age Histogram')
6.  plt.hist(data["Age"])
```

Output:

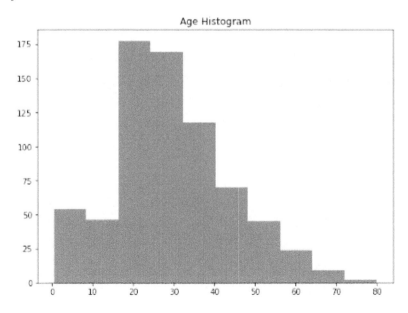

The output shows that the majority of the passengers (175) were aged between 20 and 25. Similarly, the passengers aged between 70 and 80 are least in number. By default, the age is distributed into 10 bins or 10 groups.

Further Readings – Matplotlib Histogram

To study more about Matplotlib histograms, please check Matplotlib's official documentation for histograms (https://bit.ly/30Elw3V). Get used to searching and reading this documentation. It is a great resource of knowledge.

5.2.7. Pie Charts

Pie charts, as the name suggests, display the percentage distribution of values in a categorical column in terms of an aggregated function. For instance, the following script shows the percentage distribution of jobs with respect to job categories, i.e., IT, Marketing, Data Science, and Finance. To plot a pie chart, the pie() method of the pyplot module is used. The first parameter is the list of the numeric values that you want converted and displayed into percentages. Next, you have to pass a list of categories to the labels parameter. The explode parameter defines the magnitude of the split for each category in the pie chart. The autopct parameter defines the format in which the percentage will be displayed on the pie chart.

Script 17:

```
1. labels = 'IT', 'Marketing', 'Data Science', 'Finance'
2. values = [500, 156, 300, 510]
3. explode = (0.05, 0.05, 0.05, 0.05)
4.
5. plt.pie(values, explode=explode, labels=labels,
   autopct='%1.1f%%', shadow=True)
6. plt.show()
```

Output:

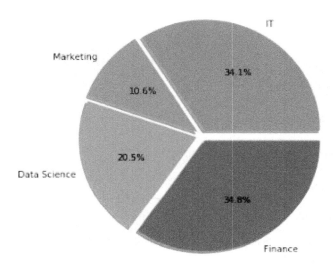

Further Readings – Matplotlib Pie Charts

To study more about Matplotlib pie charts, please check Matplotlib's official documentation for Pie Charts (https:// bit.ly/31qoXdy). Get used to searching and reading this documentation. It is a great resource of knowledge.

5.3. Data Visualization via Seaborn

In the previous section, you saw how to plot different types of graphs using Python's Matplotlib library. In this section, you will see how to perform data visualization with Seaborn, which is yet another extremely handy Python library for data visualization. The Seaborn library is based on the Matplotlib library. Therefore, you will also need to import the Matplotlib library.

To install the seaborn library, you simply have to execute the following command at your command terminal:

```
$ pip install seaborn
```

Before you start plotting different types of plot, you need to import a few libraries. The following script does that:

Script 18:

```
1. import matplotlib.pyplot as plt
2. import seaborn as sns
3.
4. plt.rcParams["figure.figsize"] = [10,8]
5.
6. tips_data = sns.load_dataset('tips')
7.
8. tips_data.head()
```

The above script imports the Matplotlib and Seaborn libraries. Next, the default plot size is increased to 10 x 8. After that, the **load_dataset()** method of the Seaborn module is used to load the **tips** dataset. Finally, the first five records of the **tips** dataset have been displayed on the console. Here is the output:

Output:

	total_bill	tip	sex	smoker	day	time	size
0	16.99	1.01	Female	No	Sun	Dinner	2
1	10.34	1.66	Male	No	Sun	Dinner	3
2	21.01	3.50	Male	No	Sun	Dinner	3
3	23.68	3.31	Male	No	Sun	Dinner	2
4	24.59	3.61	Female	No	Sun	Dinner	4

The Tips dataset contains records of the bill paid by a customer at a restaurant. The dataset contains seven columns: total_bill, tip, sex, smoker, day, time, and size. You do not have to download this dataset as it comes built-in with the Seaborn library. We will be using the **tips** dataset to plot some of the Seaborn plots. So, without any ado, let's start plotting with Seaborn.

5.3.1. The Dist Plot

The dist plot, also known as the distributional plot, is used to plot a histogram of data for a specific column in the dataset. To plot a dist plot, you can use the **distplot()** function of the Seaborn library. The name of the column for which you want to plot a histogram is passed as a parameter to the **distplot()** function. The following script plots a dist plot for the **total_bill** column of the **tips** dataset.

Script 19:

```
1. plt.rcParams["figure.figsize"] = [10,8]
2. sns.distplot(tips_data['total_bill'])
```

Output:

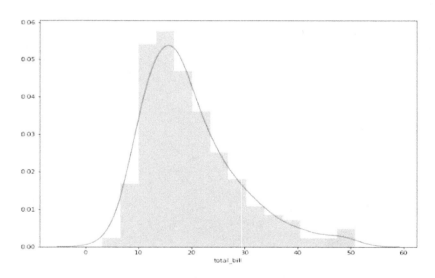

Further Readings – Seaborn Distributional Plots

To study more about Seaborn distributional plots, please check Seaborn's official documentation for distributional plots (https://bit.ly/3abHC1O). Try to plot distributional plots with a different set of attributes, as mentioned in the official documentation.

5.3.2. The Joint Plot

The joint plot is used to plot the histogram distribution of two columns, one on the x-axis and the other on the y-axis. A scatter plot is by default drawn for the points in the two columns. To plot a joint plot, you need to call the **jointplot()** function. The following script plots a joint plot for **total_bill** and **tip** columns of the **tips** dataset.

Script 20:

```
sns.jointplot(x='total_bill', y='tip', data=tips_data)
```

Output:

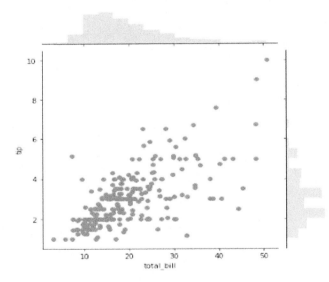

The scatter plot can be replaced by a regression line in a joint plot. To do so, you need to pass **reg** as the value for the kind parameter of the **jointplot()** function.

Script 21:

```
sns.jointplot(x='size', y='total_bill', data=tips_data,
kind = 'reg')
```

Output:

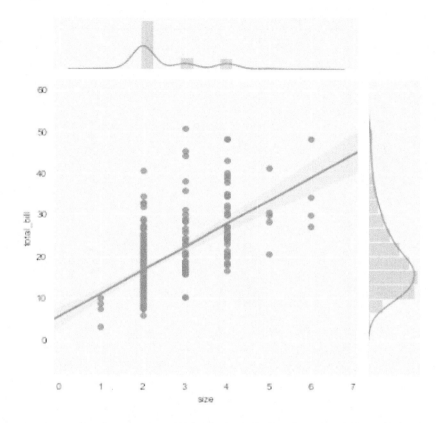

Further Readings – Seaborn Joint Plots

To study more about Seaborn joint plots, please check Seaborn's official documentation for jointplots (https://bit. ly/31DHFyO). Try to plot joint plots with a different set of attributes, as mentioned in the official documentation.

5.3.3. The Pair Plot

The pair plot is used to plot a joint plot for all the combinations of numeric and Boolean columns in a dataset. To plot a pair plot, you need to call the **pairplot()** function and pass it to your dataset.

Script 22:

```
sns.pairplot(data=tips_data)
```

Output:

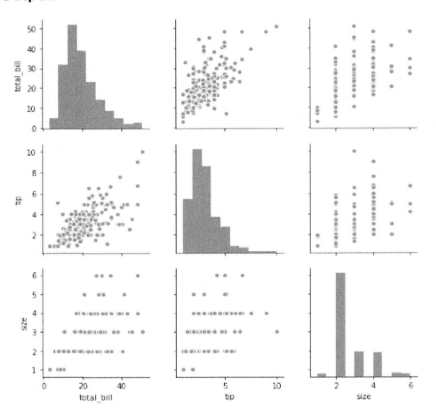

Further Readings – Seaborn Pair Plot
To study more about Seaborn pair plots, please check Seaborn's official documentation for pairplots (https://bit. ly/3a7PdgK). Try to plot pair plots with a different set of attributes, as mentioned in the official documentation.

5.3.4. The Bar Plot

The bar plot is used to capture the relationship between a categorical and numerical column. For each unique value in a categorical column, a bar is plotted, which by default, displays the mean value for the data in a numeric column specified by the bar plot.

In the following script, we first import the built-in Titanic dataset from the Seaborn library via the **load_dataset()** function. You can also read the CSV file named titanic_data. csv from the *Datasets* folder in the GitHub repository.

Script 23:

```
1.  import matplotlib.pyplot as plt
2.  import seaborn as sns
3.
4.  plt.rcParams["figure.figsize"] = [8,6]
5.  sns.set_style("darkgrid")
6.
7.  titanic_data = sns.load_dataset('titanic')
8.
9.  titanic_data.head()
```

Here are the first five rows of the Titanic dataset.

Output:

	survived	pclass	sex	age	sibsp	parch	fare	embarked	class	who	adult_male	deck	embark_town	alive	alone
0	0	3	male	22.0	1	0	7.2500	S	Third	man	True	NaN	Southampton	no	False
1	1	1	female	38.0	1	0	71.2833	C	First	woman	False	C	Cherbourg	yes	False
2	1	3	female	26.0	0	0	7.9250	S	Third	woman	False	NaN	Southampton	yes	True
3	1	1	female	35.0	1	0	53.1000	S	First	woman	False	C	Southampton	yes	False
4	0	3	male	35.0	0	0	8.0500	S	Third	man	True	NaN	Southampton	no	True

Next, we will call the **barplot()** function from the Seaborn library to plot a bar plot that displays the average age of passengers traveling in the different classes of the Titanic ship.

Script 24:

```
sns.barplot(x='pclass', y='age', data=titanic_data)
```

Output:

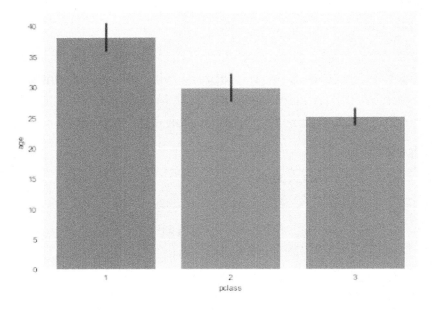

The output shows that the average age of passengers traveling in the first class is between 35 and 40. The average age of the passengers traveling in the second class is around 30, while the passengers traveling in the 3rd class have an average age of 25.

Further Readings – Seaborn Bar Plot

To study more about Seaborn bar plots, please check Seaborn's official documentation for bar plots (https://bit. ly/2Dw5DDO). Try to plot bar plots with a different set of attributes, as mentioned in the official documentation.

5.3.5. The Count Plot

The count plot plots a plot like a bar plot. However, unlike a bar plot that plots average values, the count plot simply displays the counts of the occurrences of records for each unique value in a categorical column. The **countplot()** function is used to plot a count plot with Seaborn. The following script plots a count plot for the **pclass** column of the **Titanic** dataset.

Script 25:

```
sns.countplot(x='pclass', data=titanic_data)
```

The output shows that around 200 passengers traveled in the first class, while an overwhelming majority of passengers traveled in the 3rd class of the Titanic ship.

Output:

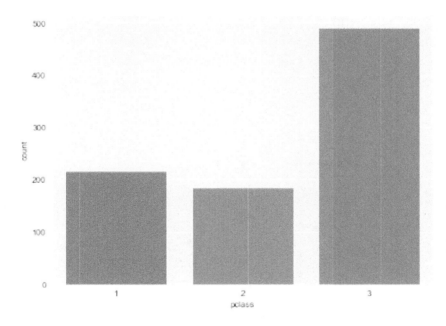

Further Readings – Seaborn Count Plot

To study more about Seaborn count plots, please check Seaborn's official documentation for count plots (https:// bit.ly/3ilzH3N). Try to plot count plots with a different set of attributes, as mentioned in the official documentation.

5.3.6. The Box Plot

The box plot is used to plot the quartile information for data in a numeric column. To plot a box plot, the **boxplot()** method is used. To plot a horizontal box plot, the column name of the dataset is passed to the x-axis. The following script plots a box plot for the **fare** column of the **Titanic** dataset.

Script 26:

```
sns.boxplot(x=titanic_data["fare"])
```

Output:

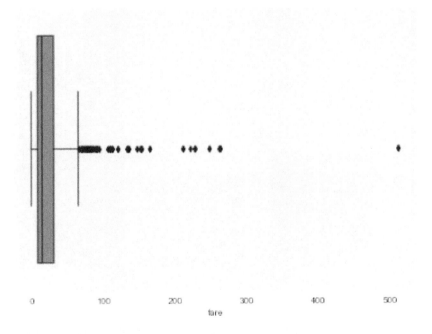

Further Readings – Seaborn Box Plot

To study more about Seaborn box plots, please check Seaborn's official documentation for box plots (https://bit.ly/3kpH4Jw). Try to plot box plots with a different set of attributes, as mentioned in the official documentation.

5.3.7. The Violin Plot

Violin plots are similar to Box plots. However, unlike Box plots that plot quartile information, the Violin plots plot the overall distribution of values in the numeric columns. The following script plots two Violin plots for the passengers traveling alone and for the passengers traveling along with another passenger. The **violinplot()** function is used to plot a swarm plot with Seaborn.

Script 27:

```
sns.violinplot(x='alone', y='age', data=titanic_data)
```

Here is the output of the above script.

Output:

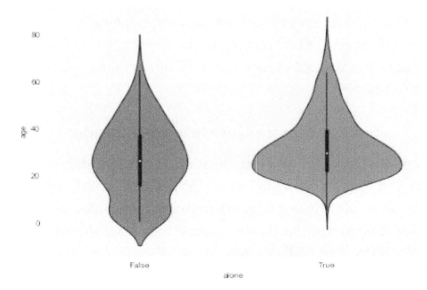

The output shows that among the passengers traveling alone, the passengers whose age is less than 15 are very few, as shown by the orange violin plot on the right. This behavior is understandable as children are normally accompanied by someone. This can be further verified by looking at the blue violin plot on the left that corresponds to the passengers accompanied by other passengers.

The hue attribute can also be used to categorize the violin plot further.

Further Readings – Seaborn Violin Plot

To study more about Seaborn violin plots, please check Seaborn's official documentation for Violin plots (https:// bit.ly/30F0qT9). Try to plot violin plots with a different set of attributes, as mentioned in the official documentation.

5.4. Data Visualization via Pandas

In the previous section, you saw how to plot different types of plots with the Seaborn library. In this chapter, you will see how the Pandas library can be used to plot different types of visualizations. As a matter of fact, the Pandas library is probably the easiest library for data plotting, as you will see in this chapter.

5.4.1. Loading Datasets with Pandas

Before you can plot any visualization with the Pandas library, you need to read data into a Pandas dataframe. The best way to do so is via the **read_csv()** method. The following script shows how to read the Titanic dataset into a dataframe named **titanic_data.** You can give any name to the dataframe.

Script 28:

```
1.  import pandas as pd
2.  titanic_data = pd.read_csv(r"E:\
    Data Visualization with Python\Datasets\titanic_data.csv")
3.  titanic_data.head()
```

Output:

	PassengerId	Survived	Pclass	Name	Sex	Age	SibSp	Parch	Ticket	Fare	Cabin	Embarked
0	1	0	3	Braund, Mr. Owen Harris	male	22.0	1.	0	A/5 21171	7.2500	NaN	S
1	2	1	1	Cumings, Mrs. John Bradley (Florence Briggs Th...	female	38.0	1	0	PC 17599	71.2833	C85	C
2	3	1	3	Heikkinen, Miss. Laina	female	26.0	0	0	STON/O2. 3101282	7.9250	NaN	S
3	4	1	1	Futrelle, Mrs. Jacques Heath (Lily May Peel)	female	35.0	1	0	113803	53.1000	C123	S
4	5	0	3	Allen, Mr. William Henry	male	35.0	0	0	373450	8.0500	NaN	S

5.4.2. Plotting Histograms with Pandas

Let's now see how to plot different types of plots with Pandas dataframe. The first plot we are going to plot is a Histogram. There are multiple ways to plot a graph in Pandas. The first way is to select the dataframe column by specifying the name of the column in square brackets that follows the dataframe name and then append the plot name via dot operator. The following script plots a histogram for the Age column of the Titanic dataset using the **hist()** function. It is important to mention that behind the scenes, the Pandas library makes use of the Matplotlib plotting functions. Therefore, you need to import the **Matplotlib's pyplot** module before you can plot Pandas visualizations.

Script 29:

```
1. import matplotlib.pyplot as plt
2. titanic_data['Age'].hist()
```

Output:

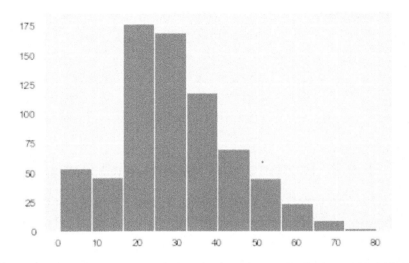

Further Readings – Pandas Histogram
To study more about the Pandas histogram, please check Pandas' official documentation for histogram (https://bit.ly/3OFOqT9). Try to execute the histogram method with a different set of attributes, as mentioned in the official documentation.

5.4.3. Pandas Line Plots

To plot line plots via the Pandas dataframe, we will use the Flights dataset. The following script imports the Flights dataset from the built-in seaborn library.

Script 30:

```
1. flights_data = sns.load_dataset('flights')
2.
3. flights_data.head()
```

Output:

	year	month	passengers
0	1949	January	112
1	1949	February .	118
2	1949	March	132
3	1949	April	129
4	1949	May	121

By default, the index serves as the x-axis. In the above script, the leftmost column, i.e., the column containing 0,1,2 … is the index column. To plot a line plot, you have to specify the column names for x and y axes. If you only specify the column value for the y-axis, the index is used as the x-axis. The following script plots a line plot for the **passengers** column of the **flights** data.

Script 31:

```
flights_data.plot.line( y='passengers', figsize=(8,6))
```

Output:

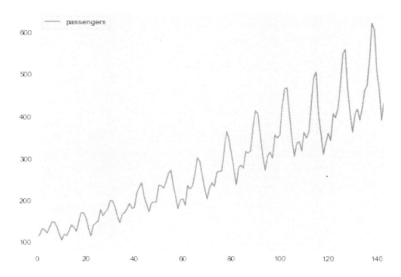

Further Readings – Pandas Line Plots

To study more about Pandas line plots, please check Pandas'
official documentation for line plots (https://bit.ly/3OFOqT9).
Try to execute the line() method with a different set of
attributes, as mentioned in the official documentation.

5.4.4. Pandas Scatter Plots

The **scatter()** function is used to plot scatter plots with Pandas.
The following script plots a scatter plot containing the year on
the x-axis and the number of passengers on the y-axis.

Script 32:

```
flights_data.plot.
scatter(x='year', y='passengers', figsize=(8,6))
```

Output:

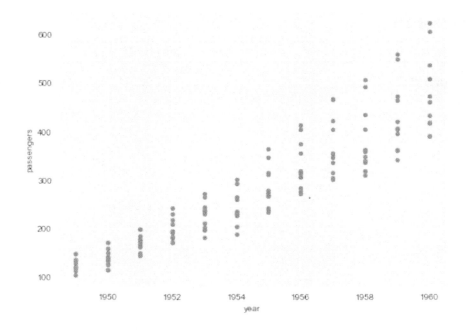

Further Readings – Pandas Scatter Plots
To study more about Pandas scatter plots, please check
Pandas' official documentation for scatter plots (https://
bit.ly/2DxSg6b). Try to execute the scatter() method with
a different set of attributes, as mentioned in the official
documentation.

5.4.5. Pandas Bar Plots

To plot Bar plots with Pandas, you need a list of categories
and a list of values. The list of categories and the list of values
must have the same length. Let's plot a bar plot that shows
the average age of male and female passengers.

To do so, we start by first calculating the mean age of both male
and female passengers traveling in the unfortunate Titanic
ship. The **groupby()** method of the Pandas dataframe can be
used to apply aggregate function with respect to categorical
columns. The following script returns the mean values for the
ages of male and female passengers for the Titanic ship.

Script 33:

```
1. titanic_data = pd.read_csv(r"E:\
   Data Visualization with Python\Datasets\titanic_data.csv")
2. titanic_data.head()
3. sex_mean = titanic_data.groupby("Sex")["Age"].mean()
4.
5. print(sex_mean)
6. print(type(sex_mean.tolist()))
```

Output:

```
Sex
female    27.915709
male      30.726645
Name: Age, dtype: float64
<class 'list'>
```

Next, we need to create a new Pandas dataframe with two columns: Gender and Age, and then we can simply use the **bar()** method to plot a bar plot that displays the average ages of male and female passengers on the Titanic ship.

Script 34:

```
1.  df = pd.DataFrame({'Gender':['Female', 'Male'], 'Age':sex_
    mean.tolist()})
2.  ax = df.plot.bar(x='Gender', y='Age', figsize=(8,6))
```

Output:

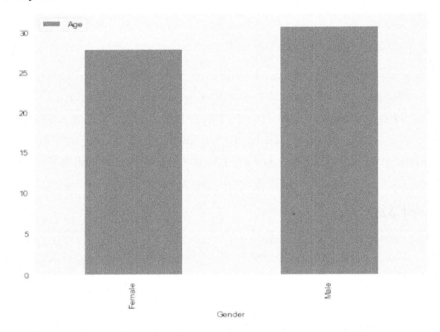

Further Readings – Pandas Bar Plots

To study more about Pandas bar plots, please check Pandas' official documentation for bar plots (https://bit.ly/31uCe5a). Try to execute bar plot methods with a different set of attributes, as mentioned in the official documentation.

5.4.6. Pandas Box Plots

To plot box plots via the Pandas library, you need to call the **box()** function. The following script plots box plots for all the numeric columns in the Titanic dataset.

Output:

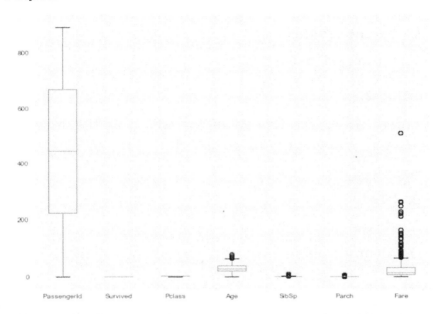

Further Readings – Pandas Box Plots

To study more about Pandas box plots, please check Pandas' official documentation for box plots (https://bit.ly/3kAvRWG). Try to execute box plot methods with a different set of attributes, as mentioned in the official documentation.

Exercise 5.1

Question 1

Which Pandas function is used to plot a horizontal bar plot:

A. horz_bar()

B. barh()

C. bar_horizontal()

D. horizontal_bar()

Question 2:

To create a legend, the value for which of the following parameters is needed to be specified?

A. title

B. label

C. axis

D. All of the above

Question 3:

How to show percentage values on a Matplotlib Pie Chart?

A. autopct = '%1.1f%%'

B. percentage = '%1.1f%%'

C. perc = '%1.1f%%'

D. None of the Above

Exercise 5.2

Plot two scatter plots on the same graph using the tips_ dataset. In the first scatter plot, display values from the total_ bill column on the x-axis and from the tip column on the y-axis. The color of the first scatter plot should be green. In the second scatter plot, display values from the total_bill column on the x-axis and from the size column on the y-axis. The color of the second scatter plot should be blue, and markers should be x.

Solving Regression Problems in Machine Learning Using Sklearn Library

Machine learning is a branch of artificial intelligence that enables computer programs to automatically learn and improve from experience. Machine learning algorithms learn from datasets, and then based on the patterns identified from the datasets, make predictions on unseen data.

Machine learning algorithms can be mainly categorized into two types: supervised learning algorithms and unsupervised learning algorithms.

Supervised machine learning algorithms are those algorithms where the input dataset and the corresponding output or true prediction are available, and the algorithms try to find the relationship between the inputs and outputs.

In unsupervised machine learning algorithms, however, the true labels for the outputs are not known. Rather, the algorithms try to find similar patterns in the data. Clustering algorithms are a typical example of unsupervised learning.

Supervised learning algorithms are divided further into two types: regression algorithms and classification algorithms.

Regression algorithms predict a continuous value, for example, the price of a house, blood pressure of a person, and a student's score in a particular exam. Classification algorithms, on the flip side, predict a discrete value such as whether or not a tumor is malignant, whether a student is going to pass or fail an exam, etc.

In this chapter, you will study how machine learning algorithms can be used to solve regression problems, i.e., predict a continuous value using the Sklearn library (https://bit.ly/2Zvy2Sm). In chapter 7, you will see how to solve classification problems via Sklearn. The 8th chapter gives an overview of the unsupervised learning algorithm.

6.1. Preparing Data for Regression Problems

Machine learning algorithms require data to be in a certain format before the algorithms can be trained on the data. In this section, you will see various data preprocessing steps that you need to perform before you can train machine learning algorithms using the Sklearn library.

You can read data from CSV files. However, the datasets we are going to use in this section are available by default in the Seaborn library. To view all the datasets, you can use the get_dataset_names() function as shown in the following script:

Script 1:

```
1.  import pandas as pd
2.  import numpy as np
3.  import seaborn as sns
4.  sns.get_dataset_names()
```

Output:

```
['anagrams',
 'anscombe',
 'attention',
 'brain_networks',
 'car_crashes',
 'diamonds',
 'dots',
 'exercise',
 'flights',
 'fmri',
 'gammas',
 'geyser',
 'iris',
 'mpg',
 'penguins',
 'planets',
 'tips',
 'titanic']
```

To read a particular dataset into the Pandas dataframe, pass the dataset name to the load_dataset() method of the Seaborn library.

The following script loads the *Tips* dataset and displays its first five rows.

Script 2:

```
1. tips_df = sns.load_dataset("tips")
2. tips_df.head()
```

Output:

	total_bill	tip	sex	smoker	day	time	size
0	16.99	1.01	Female	No	Sun	Dinner	2
1	10.34	1.66	Male	No	Sun	Dinner	3
2	21.01	3.50	Male	No	Sun	Dinner	3
3	23.68	3.31	Male	No	Sun	Dinner	2
4	24.59	3.61	Female	No	Sun	Dinner	4

Similarly, the following script loads the *Diamonds* dataset and displays its first five rows.

Script 3:

```
1. diamond_df = sns.load_dataset("diamonds")
2. diamond_df.head()
```

Output:

	carat	cut	color	clarity	depth	table	price	x	y	z
0	0.23	Ideal	E	SI2	61.5	55.0	326	3.95	3.98	2.43
1	0.21	Premium	E	SI1	59.8	61.0	326	3.89	3.84	2.31
2	0.23	Good	E	VS1	56.9	65.0	327	4.05	4.07	2.31
3	0.29	Premium	I	VS2	62.4	58.0	334	4.20	4.23	2.63
4	0.31	Good	J	SI2	63.3	58.0	335	4.34	4.35	2.75

In this chapter, we will be working with the Tips dataset. We will be using machine learning algorithms to predict the "tip" for a particular record, based on the remaining features such as "total_bill," "sex," "day," "time," etc.

6.1.1. Dividing Data into Features and Labels

As a first step, we divide the data into features and labels sets. Our labels set consists of values from the "tip" column, while the features set consists of values from the remaining columns. The following script divides the data into features and labels sets.

Script 4:

```
1. X = tips_df.drop(['tip'], axis=1)
2. y = tips_df["tip"]
```

Let's print the feature set.

Script 5:

```
1. X.head()
```

Output:

	total_bill	sex	smoker	day	time	size
0	16.99	Female	No	Sun	Dinner	2
1	10.34	Male	No	Sun	Dinner	3
2	21.01	Male	No	Sun	Dinner	3
3	23.68	Male	No	Sun	Dinner	2
4	24.59	Female	No	Sun	Dinner	4

And the following script prints the label set.

Script 6:

```
1. y.head()
```

Output:

```
0      1.01
1      1.66
2      3.50
3      3.31
4      3.61
Name: tip, dtype: float64
```

6.1.2. Converting Categorical Data to Numbers

Machine learning algorithms, for the most part, can only work with numbers. Therefore, it is important to convert categorical data into a numeric format.

In this regard, the first step is to create a dataset of all numeric values. To do so, drop the categorical columns from the dataset, as shown below.

Script 7:

```
numerical = X.drop(['sex', 'smoker', 'day', 'time'], axis = 1)
```

The output below shows that the dataframe "numerical" contains numeric columns only.

Script 8:

```
1.  numerical.head()
```

Output:

	total_bill	size
0	16.99	2
1	10.34	3
2	21.01	3
3	23.68	2
4	24.59	4

Next, you need to create a dataframe that contains only categorical columns.

Script 9:

```
1.  categorical = X.filter(['sex', 'smoker', 'day', 'time'])
2.  categorical.head()
```

Output:

	sex	smoker	day	time
0	Female	No	Sun	Dinner
1	Male	No	Sun	Dinner
2	Male	No	Sun	Dinner
3	Male	No	Sun	Dinner
4	Female	No	Sun	Dinner

One of the most common approaches to convert a categorical column to a numeric one is via one-hot encoding. In one-hot encoding, for every unique value in the original columns, a new column is created. For instance, for sex, two columns: Female and Male, are created. If the original sex column contained male, a 1 is added in the newly created Male column, while 1 is added in the newly created Female column if the original sex column contained female.

However, it can be noted that we do not really need two columns. A single column, i.e., Female is enough since when a customer is female, we can add 1 in the Female column, else 1 can be added in that column. Hence, we need N-1 one-hot encoded columns for all the N values in the original column.

The following script converts categorical columns into one-hot encoded columns using the pd.get_dummies() method.

Script 10:

```
1.  import pandas as pd
2.  cat_numerical = pd.get_dummies(categorical,drop_first=True)
3.  cat_numerical.head()
```

The output shows the newly created one-hot encoded columns.

Output:

	sex_Female	smoker_No	day_Fri	day_Sat	day_Sun	time_Dinner
0	1	1	0	0	1	1
1	0	1	0	0	1	1
2	0	1	0	0	1	1
3	0	1	0	0	1	1
4	1	1	0	0	1	1

The final step is to join the numerical columns with the one-hot encoded columns. To do so, you can use the concat() function from the Pandas library as shown below:

Script 11:

```
1. X = pd.concat([numerical, cat_numerical], axis = 1)
2. X.head()
```

The final dataset looks like this. You can see that it doesn't contain any categorical value.

Output:

	total_bill	size	sex_Female	smoker_No	day_Fri	day_Sat	day_Sun	time_Dinner
0	16.99	2	1	1	0	0	1	1
1	10.34	3	0	1	0	0	1	1
2	21.01	3	0	1	0	0	1	1
3	23.68	2	0	1	0	0	1	1
4	24.59	4	1	1	0	0	1	1

6.1.3. Divide Data into Training and Test Sets

After you train a machine learning algorithm, you need to evaluate it to see how well it performs on unseen data. Therefore, we divide the dataset into two sets, i.e., a training set and a test set. The dataset is trained via the training set and evaluated on the test set. To split the data into training and test sets, you can use the train_test_split() function from the Sklearn library, as shown below. The following script divides the data into an 80 percent training set and a 20 percent test set.

Script 12:

```
1. from sklearn.model_selection import train_test_split
2.
3. X_train, X_test, y_train, y_test = train_test_
   split(X, y,  test_size=0.20, random_state=0)
```

6.1.4. Data Scaling/Normalization

The final step (optional) before the data is passed to machine learning algorithms is to scale the data. You can see that some columns of the dataset contain small values, while the others contain very large values. It is better to convert all values to a uniform scale. To do so, you can use the StandardScaler() function from the sklearn.preprocessing module, as shown below:

Script 13:

```
1.  from sklearn.preprocessing import StandardScaler
2.  sc = StandardScaler()
3.  #scaling the training set
4.  X_train = sc.fit_transform(X_train)
5.  #scaling the test set
6.  X_test = sc.transform (X_test)
```

We have converted the data into a format that can be used to train machine learning algorithms for regression from the Sklearn library. The details, including functionalities and usage of all the machine learning algorithms, are available at this link. You can check all the regression algorithms by going to that link.

In the following section, we will review some of the most commonly used regression algorithms.

6.2. Linear Regression

Linear regression is a linear model that presumes a linear relationship between inputs and outputs and minimizes the cost of error between the predicted and actual output using functions like mean absolute error between different data points.

Why Use Linear Regression Algorithm?

The random forest algorithm is particularly useful when:

1. Linear regression is a simple to implement and easily interpretable algorithm.

2. Takes less training time to train even for huge datasets.

3. Linear regression coefficients are easy to interpret.

Disadvantages of Linear Regression Algorithm

The following are the disadvantages of the linear regression algorithm.

1. Performance is easily affected by outlier presence.

2. Assumes a linear relationship between dependent and independent variables, which can result in an increased error.

Implementing Linear Regression with Sklearn

To implement linear regression with Sklearn, you can use the LinearRegression class from the sklearn.linear_model module. To train the algorithm, the training and test sets, i.e., X_train and X_test in our case, are passed to the fit() method of the object of the LinearRegression class. The test set is passed to the predict() method of the class to make predictions. The process of training and making predictions with the linear regression algorithm is as follows:

Script 14:

```
1. from sklearn.linear_model import LinearRegression
2. # training the algorithm
3. lin_reg = LinearRegression()
4. regressor = lin_reg.fit(X_train, y_train)
5. # making predictions on test set
6. y_pred = regressor.predict(X_test)
```

Once you have trained a model and have made predictions on the test set, the next step is to know how well has your model performed for making predictions on the unknown test set. There are various metrics to check that. However, mean absolute error, mean squared error, and root mean squared error are three of the most common metrics.

Mean Absolute Error

Mean absolute error (MAE) is calculated by taking the average of absolute error obtained by subtracting real values from predicted values. The equation for calculating MAE is:

$$MAE = \frac{\sum_{i=1}^{n}|y_i - \hat{y}_1|}{n}$$

Mean Squared Error

Mean squared error (MSE) is similar to MAE. However, error for each record is squared in the case of MSE in order to punish data records with a huge difference between predicted and actual values. The equation to calculate the mean squared error is as follows:

$$MSE = \frac{1}{n}\sum_{i=1}^{n}(y_i - \hat{y})^2$$

Root Mean Squared Error

Root Mean Squared Error is simply the under root of mean squared error and can be calculated as follows:

$$RMSE = \sqrt{\frac{1}{n}\sum_{i=1}^{n}(y_i - \hat{y})^2}$$

The methods used to find the value for these metrics are available in sklearn.metrics class. The predicted and actual values have to be passed to these methods, as shown in the output.

Script 15:

```
1. from sklearn import metrics
2.
3. print('Mean Absolute Error:', metrics.mean_absolute_
   error(y_test, y_pred))
4. print('Mean Squared Error:', metrics.mean_squared_error(y_
   test, y_pred))
5. print('Root Mean Squared Error:', np.sqrt(metrics.mean_
   squared_error(y_test, y_pred)))
```

Here is the output. By looking at the mean absolute error, it can be concluded that on average, there is an error of 0.70 for predictions, which means that on average, the predicted tip values are 0.70$ more or less than the actual tip values.

Output:

```
Mean Absolute Error: 0.7080218832979829
Mean Squared Error: 0.893919522160961
Root Mean Squared Error: 0.9454731736865732
```

Further Readings – Linear Regression

To study more about linear regression, please check these links:
1. https://bit.ly/2ZyCa49
2. https://bit.ly/2RmLhAp

6.3. KNN Regression

KNN stands for K-nearest neighbors. KNN is a lazy learning algorithm, which is based on finding Euclidean distance between different data points.

Why Use KNN Algorithm?

The KNN is particularly useful when:

1. KNN Algorithm doesn't assume any relationship between the features.
2. Useful for a dataset where data localization is important.
3. Only have to tune the parameter K, which is the number of nearest neighbors.
4. No training is needed, as it is a lazy learning algorithm.
5. Recommender systems and finding semantic similarity between the documents are major applications of the KNN algorithm.

Disadvantages of the KNN Algorithm

The following are the disadvantages of KNN algorithm.

1. You have to find the optimal value for K, which is not easy.
2. Not suitable for very high dimensional data.

Implementing the KNN Algorithm with SKlearn

With Sklearn, it is extremely easy to implement KNN regression. To do so, you can use the KNeighborsRegressor class. The process of training and testing is the same as linear regression. For training, you need to call the fit() method, and for testing, you need to call the predict() method.

The following script shows the process of training, testing, and evaluating the KNN regression algorithm for predicting the values for the tip column from the Tips dataset.

Script 16:

```
1.  from sklearn.neighbors import KNeighborsRegressor
2.  knn_reg = KNeighborsRegressor(n_neighbors=5)
3.  regressor = knn_reg.fit(X_train, y_train)
4.
5.  y_pred = regressor.predict(X_test)
6.
7.
8.  from sklearn import metrics
9.
10. print('Mean Absolute Error:', metrics.mean_absolute_error(y_test, y_
    pred))
11. print('Mean Squared Error:', metrics.mean_squared_error(y_test, y_
    pred))
12. print('Root Mean Squared Error:', np.sqrt(metrics.mean_squared_
    error(y_test, y_pred)))
```

Output:

```
Mean Absolute Error: 0.7513877551020406
Mean Squared Error: 0.9462902040816326
Root Mean Squared Error: 0.9727744877830794
```

Further Readings – KNN Regression

To study more about KNN regression, please check these links:

1. https://bit.ly/35sluOM
2. https://bit.ly/33r2Zbq

6.4. Random Forest Regression

Random forest is a tree-based algorithm that converts features into tree nodes and then uses entropy loss to make predictions.

Why Use Random Forest Algorithms?

Random forest algorithms are particularly useful when:

1. You have lots of missing data or an imbalanced dataset.

2. With large number of trees, you can avoid overfitting while training. Overfitting occurs when machine learning models perform better on the training set but worse on the test set.

3. The random forest algorithm can be used when you have very high dimensional data.

4. Through cross-validation, the random forest algorithm can return higher accuracy.

5. The random forest algorithm can solve both classification and regression tasks and finds its application in a variety of tasks ranging from credit card fraud detection, stock market prediction, and finding fraudulent online transactions.

Disadvantages of Random Forest Algorithms

There are two major disadvantages of Random forest algorithms:

1. Using a large number of trees can slow down the algorithm.

2. Random forest algorithm is a predictive algorithm, which can only predict the future and cannot explain what happened in the past using the dataset.

Implementing Random Forest Regressor Using Sklearn

RandomForestRegressor class from the Sklearn.ensemble module can be used to implement random forest regressor algorithms, as shown below.

Script 17:

```
1.  # training and testing the random forest
2.  from sklearn.ensemble import RandomForestRegressor
3.  rf_reg = RandomForestRegressor(random_state=42, n_
    estimators=500)
4.  regressor = rf_reg.fit(X_train, y_train)
5.  y_pred = regressor.predict(X_test)
6.
7.  # evaluating algorithm performance
8.  from sklearn import metrics
9.
10. print('Mean Absolute Error:', metrics.mean_absolute_
    error(y_test, y_pred))
11. print('Mean Squared Error:', metrics.mean_squared_error(y_
    test, y_pred))
12. print('Root Mean Squared Error:', np.sqrt(metrics.mean_
    squared_error(y_test, y_pred)))
```

The mean absolute error value of 0.70 shows that random forest performs better than both linear regression and KNN for predicting tip in the Tips dataset.

Output:

```
Mean Absolute Error: 0.7054065306122449
Mean Squared Error: 0.8045782841306138
Root Mean Squared Error: 0.8969828783932354
```

Further Readings – Random Forest Regression

To study more about Random Forest Regression, please check these links:

1. https://bit.ly/3bRkKEy
2. https://bit.ly/35u3BzH

6.5. Support Vector Regression

The support vector machine is classification as well as regression algorithms, which minimizes the error between the actual predictions and predicted predictions by maximizing the distance between hyperplanes that contain data for various records.

Why Use SVR Algorithms?

Support Vector Regression is a support vector machine (SVM) variant for regression. SVM has the following usages.

1. It can be used to perform regression or classification with high dimensional data.

2. With the kernel trick, SVM is capable of applying regression and classification to non-linear datasets.

3. SVM algorithms are commonly used for ordinal classification or regression, and this is why they are commonly known as ranking algorithms.

Disadvantages of SVR Algorithms

There are three major disadvantages of SVR algorithms:

1. Lots of parameters to be optimized in order to get the best performance.

2. Training can take a long time on large datasets.

3. Yields poor results if the number of features is greater than the number of records in a dataset.

Implementing SVR Using Sklearn

With the Sklearn library, you can use the SVM class to implement support vector regression algorithms, as shown below.

Script 18:

```
1.  # training and testing the SVM
2.
3.  from sklearn import svm
4.  svm_reg = svm.SVR()
5.
6.  regressor = svm_reg.fit(X_train, y_train)
7.  y_pred = regressor.predict(X_test)
8.
9.
10. from sklearn import metrics
11.
12. print('Mean Absolute Error:', metrics.mean_absolute_
    error(y_test, y_pred))
13. print('Mean Squared Error:', metrics.mean_squared_error(y_
    test, y_pred))
14. print('Root Mean Squared Error:', np.sqrt(metrics.mean_
    squared_error(y_test, y_pred)))
```

```
Mean Absolute Error: 0.7362521512772694
Mean Squared Error: 0.9684825097223093
Root Mean Squared Error: 0.9841150896731079
```

Further Readings – Support Vector Regression

To study more about support vector regression, please
check these links:
1. https://bit.ly/3bRACH9
2. https://bit.ly/3mg5PZG

Which Model to Use?

The results obtained from section 6.2 to 6.5 shows that
Random Forest Regressor algorithms result in the minimum
MAE, MSE, and RMSE values. The algorithm you choose to
use depends totally upon your dataset and evaluation metrics.
Some algorithms perform better on one dataset while other
algorithms perform better on the other dataset. It is better
that you use all the algorithms to see, which gives the best

results. However, if you have limited options, it is best to start with ensemble learning algorithms such as Random Forest. They yield the best result.

6.6. K Fold Cross-Validation

Earlier, we divided the data into an 80 Percent training set and a 20 percent test set. However, it means that only 20 percent of the data is used for testing and that 20 percent of data is never used for training.

For more stable results, it is recommended that all the parts of the dataset are used at least once for training and once for testing. The K-Fold cross-validation technique can be used to do so. With K-fold cross-validation, the data is divided into K parts. The experiments are also performed for K parts. In each experiment, K-1 parts are used for training, and the Kth part is used for testing.

For example, in 5-fold cross-validation, the data is divided into five equal parts, e.g., K1, K2, K3, K4, and K5. In the first iteration, K1–K4 are used for training, while K5 is used for testing. In the second test, K1, K2, K3, and K5 are used for training, and K4 is used for testing. In this way, each part is used at least once for testing and once for training.

You can use cross_val_score() function from the sklearn.model_selection module to perform cross validation as shown below:

Script 19:

```
1.  from sklearn.model_selection import cross_val_score
2.
3.  print(cross_val_score(regressor, X, y, cv=5, scoring ="neg_
    mean_absolute_error"))
```

Output:

```
[-0.66386205 -0.57007269 -0.63598762 -0.96960743 -0.87391702]
```

The output shows the mean absolute value for each of the K folds.

6.7. Making Prediction on a Single Record

In the previous sections, you saw how to make predictions on a complete test set. In this section, you will see how to make a prediction using a single record as an input.

Let's pick the 100th record from our dataset.

Script 20:

```
1. tips_df.loc[100]
```

The output shows that the value of the tip in the 100th record in our dataset is 2.5.

Output:

```
total_bill      11.35
tip              2.5
sex            Female
smoker            Yes
day               Fri
time           Dinner
size               2
Name: 100, dtype: object
```

We will try to predict the value of the tip of the 100th record using the random forest regressor algorithm and see what output we get. Look at the script below:

Note that you have to scale your single record before it can be used as input to your machine learning algorithm.

Script 21:

```
1. from sklearn.ensemble import RandomForestRegressor
2. rf_reg = RandomForestRegressor(random_state=42, n_
   estimators=500)
3. regressor = rf_reg.fit(X_train, y_train)
4.
5. single_record = sc.transform (X.values[100].
   reshape(1, -1))
6. predicted_tip = regressor.predict(single_record)
7. print(predicted_tip)
```

Output:

```
[2.2609]
```

The predicted value of the tip is 2.26, which is pretty close to 2.5, i.e., the actual value.

In the next chapter, you will see how to solve classification problems using machine learning algorithms in Scikit (Sklearn) library.

Hands-on Time – Exercise

Now, it is your turn. Follow the instructions in **the exercises below** to check your understanding of the regression algorithms in machine learning. The answers to these exercises are provided after chapter 10 in this book.

Exercise 6.1

Question 1

Among the following, which one is an example of a regression output?

    A. True

    B. Red

    C. 2.5

    D. None of the above

Question 2

Which of the following algorithm is a lazy algorithm?

    A. Random Forest

    B. KNN

    C. SVM

    D. Linear Regression

Question 3

Which of the following algorithm is not a regression metric?

    A. Accuracy

    B. Recall

    C. F1 Measure

    D. All of the above

Exercise 6.2

Using the *Diamonds* dataset from the Seaborn library, train a regression algorithm of your choice, which predicts the price of the diamond. Perform all the preprocessing steps.

7

Solving Classification Problems in Machine Learning Using Sklearn Library

In the previous chapter, you saw how to solve regression problems with machine learning using the Sklearn library (https://bit.ly/2Zvy2Sm). In this chapter, you will see how to solve classification problems. Classification problems are the type of problems where you have to predict a discrete value, i.e., whether or not a tumor is malignant, if the condition of a car is good, whether or not a student will pass an exam, and so on.

7.1. Preparing Data for Classification Problems

Like regression, you have to first convert data into a specific format before it can be used to train classification algorithms.

The following script imports the Pandas, Seaborn, and NumPy libraries.

Script 1:

```
1. import pandas as pd
2. import numpy as np
3. import seaborn as sns
```

The following script uses the read_csv() method from the Pandas library to read the customer_churn.csv file, which contains records of customers who left the bank six months after various information about them is recorded. The head() method prints the first five rows of the dataset.

Script 2:

```
1. churn_df = pd.read_csv("E:\
   Hands on Python for Data Science and Machine Learning\
   Datasets\customer_churn.csv")
2. churn_df.head()
```

The output shows that the dataset contains information such as surname, customer id, geography, gender, age, etc., as shown below. The Exited column contains information regarding whether or not the customer exited the bank after six months.

Output:

Number	CustomerId	Surname	CreditScore	Geography	Gender	Age	Tenure	Balance	NumOfProducts	HasCrCard	IsActiveMember	EstimatedSalary	Exited
1	15634602	Hargrave	619	France	Female	42	2	0.00	1	1	1	101348.88	1
2	15647311	Hill	608	Spain	Female	41	1	83807.86	1	0	1	112542.58	0
3	15619304	Onio	502	France	Female	42	8	159660.80	3	1	0	113931.57	1
4	15701354	Boni	699	France	Female	39	1	0.00	2	0	0	93826.63	0
5	15737888	Mitchell	850	Spain	Female	43	2	125510.82	1	1	1	79084.10	0

We do not need RowNumber, CustomerId, and Surname columns in our dataset since they do not help in predicting if a customer will churn or not. To remove these columns, you can use the drop() method, as shown below:

Script 3:

```
1.  churn_df = churn_df.drop(['RowNumber', 'CustomerId',
    'Surname'], axis=1)
```

7.1.1. Dividing Data into Features and Labels

As shown in regression, the next step in classification is to divide the data into the features and labels. The features set, i.e., X in the following script contains all the columns except the Exited column. On the other hand, the labels set, i.e., y, contains values from the Exited column only.

Script 4:

```
1.  X = churn_df.drop(['Exited'], axis=1)
2.  y = churn_df['Exited']
```

The following script prints the first five rows of the feature set.

Script 5:

```
1.  X.head()
```

Output:

	CreditScore	Geography	Gender	Age	Tenure	Balance	NumOfProducts	HasCrCard	IsActiveMember	EstimatedSalary
0	619	France	Female	42	2	0.00	1	1	1	101348.88
1	608	Spain	Female	41	1	83807.86	1	0	1	112542.58
2	502	France	Female	42	8	159660.80	3	1	0	113931.57
3	699	France	Female	39	1	0.00	2	0	0	93826.63
4	850	Spain	Female	43	2	125510.82	1	1	1	79084.10

And the following script prints the first five rows of the label set, as shown below:

Script 6:

```
1.  y.head()
```

Output:

```
0    1
1    0
2    1
3    0
4    0
Name: Exited, dtype: int64
```

7.1.2. Converting Categorical Data to Numbers

In Section 6.1.2, you saw that we converted categorical columns to numerical because the machine learning algorithms in the Sklearn library only work with numbers.

For the classification problem, too, we need to convert the categorical column to numerical ones.

The first step then is to create a dataframe containing only numeric values. You can do so by dropping the categorical column and creating a new dataframe.

Script 7:

```
1.  numerical = X.drop(['Geography', 'Gender'], axis = 1)
```

The following script prints the dataframe that contains numeric columns only.

Script 8:

```
1.  numerical.head()
```

Output:

	CreditScore	Age	Tenure	Balance	NumOfProducts	HasCrCard	IsActiveMember	Estimated Salary
0	619	42	2	0.00	1	1	1	101348.88
1	608	41	1	83807.86	1	0	1	112542.58
2	502	42	8	159660.80	3	1	0	113931.57
3	699	39	1	0.00	2	0	0	93826.63
4	850	43	2	125510.82	1	1	1	79084.10

Next, create a dataframe that contains categorical values only. You can do so by using the filter() function as shown below:

Script 9:

```
1. categorical = X.filter(['Geography', 'Gender'])
2. categorical.head()
```

The output shows that there are two categorical columns: Geography and Gender in our dataset.

Output:

	Geography	Gender
0	France	Female
1	Spain	Female
2	France	Female
3	France	Female
4	Spain	Female

In the previous chapter, you saw how to use the one-hot encoding approach in order to convert categorical features to numeric ones. Here, we will use the same approach:

The following script converts categorical columns into one-hot encoded columns using the pd.get_dummies() method.

Script 10:

```
1. import pandas as pd
2. cat_numerical = pd.get_dummies(categorical,drop_first=True)
3. cat_numerical.head(
```

Output:

	Geography_Germany	Geography_Spain	Gender_Male
0	0	0	0
1	0	1	0
2	0	0	0
3	0	0	0
4	0	1	0

The last and final step is to join or concatenate the numeric columns and one-hot encoded categorical columns. To do so, you can use the concat function from the Pandas library, as shown below:

Script 11:

```
1. X = pd.concat([numerical, cat_numerical], axis = 1)
2. X.head()
```

The final dataset containing all the values in numeric form is shown here:

Output:

	CreditScore	Age	Tenure	Balance	NumOfProducts	HasCrCard	IsActiveMember	EstimatedSalary	Geography_Germany	Geography_Spain	Gender_Male
0	619	42	2	0.00	1	1	1	101348.88	0	0	0
1	608	41	1	83807.86	1	0	1	112542.58	0	1	0
2	502	42	8	159660.80	3	1	0	113931.57	0	0	0
3	699	39	1	0.00	2	0	0	93826.63	0	0	0
4	850	43	2	125510.82	1	1	1	79084.10	0	1	0

7.1.3. Divide Data into Training and Test Sets

After you train a machine learning algorithm, you need to evaluate it to see how well it performs on unseen data. Like regression, in classification problems, too, we divide the dataset into two sets, i.e., the training set and test set. The dataset is trained via the training set and evaluated on the test set. To split the data into training and test sets, you can use the train_test_split() function from the Sklearn library, as shown below. The following script divides the data into an 80 percent training set and a 20 percent test set.

Script 12:

```
1. from sklearn.model_selection import train_test_split
2. #  test size is the fraction of test size
3. X_train, X_test, y_train, y_test = train_test_
   split(X, y,  test_size=0.20, random_state=0)
```

7.1.4. Data Scaling/Normalization

The last step (optional) before data is passed to the machine learning algorithms is to scale the data. You can see that some columns of the dataset contain small values, while the other columns contain very large values. It is better to convert all values to a uniform scale. To do so, you can use the StandardScaler() function from the sklearn.preprocessing module, as shown below:

Script 13:

```
1. from sklearn.preprocessing import StandardScaler
2. sc = StandardScaler()
3. X_train = sc.fit_transform(X_train)
4. X_test = sc.transform (X_test)
```

We have converted data into a format that can be used to train machine learning algorithms for classification from the Sklearn library. The details, including functionalities and usage of all the machine learning algorithms, are available at this link. You can check all the classification algorithms by going to that link.

In the following section, we will review some of the most commonly used classification algorithms.

7.2. Logistic Regression

Logistic regression is a linear model which makes classification by passing the output of linear regression through a sigmoid function. The pros and cons of logistic regression algorithms are the same as linear regression algorithm explained already in chapter 6, section 6.2.

To implement linear regression with Sklearn, you can use the LogisticRegression class from the sklearn.linear_model module. To train the algorithm, the training and test sets, i.e., X_train and X_test in our case, are passed to the fit() method of the object of the LogisticRegression class. The test set is passed to the predict() method of the class to make predictions. The process of training and making predictions with the linear regression algorithm is as follows:

Script 14:

```
1.  from sklearn.linear_model import LogisticRegression
2.
3.  log_clf = LogisticRegression()
4.  classifier = log_clf.fit(X_train, y_train)
5.
6.  y_pred = classifier.predict(X_test)
7.
8.
```

Once you have trained a model and have made predictions on the test set, the next step is to know how well your model has performed for making predictions on the unknown test set. There are various metrics to evaluate a classification method. Some of the most commonly used classification metrics are F1, recall, precision, accuracy, and confusion matrix. Before you see the equations for these terms, you need to understand the concept of true positive, true negative, false positive, and false negative outputs:

True Negatives: (TN/tn): True negatives are those output labels that are actually false, and the model also predicted them as false.

True Positive: True positives are those labels that are actually true and also predicted as true by the model.

False Negative: False negative are labels that are actually true but predicted as false by the machine learning models.

False Positive: Labels that are actually false but predicted as true by the model are called false positive.

One way to analyze the results of a classification algorithm is by plotting a confusion matrix such as the one shown below:

Confusion Matrix

		Predicted Class	
Total Population n = a number		False (0)	True (1)
Actual Class	False (0)	TN True Negative	FP False Positive
	True (1)	FN False Negative	TP True Positive

Precision

Another way to analyze a classification algorithm is by calculating precision, which is basically obtained by dividing true positives by the sum of true positive and false positive, as shown below:

$$\text{Precision} = \frac{tp}{tp + fp}$$

Recall

Recall is calculated by dividing true positives by the sum of the true positive and false negative, as shown below:

$$\text{Recall} = \frac{tp}{tp + fn}$$

F1 Measure

F1 measure is simply the harmonic mean of precision and recall and is calculated as follows:

$$F_1 = \left(\frac{2}{\text{recall}^{-1} + \text{precision}^{-1}} \right) = 2 \cdot \frac{\text{precision} \cdot \text{recall}}{\text{precision} + \text{recall}}$$

Accuracy

Accuracy refers to the number of correctly predicted labels divided by the total number of observations in a dataset.

$$\text{Accuracy} = \frac{tp + tn}{tp + tn + fp + fn}$$

The choice of using a metric for a classification problem depends totally upon you. However, as a rule of thumb, in case of balanced datasets, i.e., where the number of labels for each class is balanced, accuracy can be used as an evaluation metric. For imbalanced datasets, you can use F1 the measure as the classification metric.

The methods used to find the value for these metrics are available in the sklearn.metrics class. The predicted and actual values have to be passed to these methods, as shown in the output.

Script 15:

```
9.  from sklearn.metrics import classification_
    report, confusion_matrix, accuracy_score
10.
11. print(confusion_matrix(y_test,y_pred))
12. print(classification_report(y_test,y_pred))
13. print(accuracy_score(y_test, y_pred))
```

Output:

```
[[1526    69]
 [ 309    96]]
              precision    recall  f1-score   support

           0       0.83      0.96      0.89      1595
           1       0.58      0.24      0.34       405

    accuracy                           0.81      2000
   macro avg       0.71      0.60      0.61      2000
weighted avg       0.78      0.81      0.78      2000

0.811
```

The output shows that for 81 percent of the records in the test set, logistic regression correctly predicted whether or not a customer will leave the bank.

Further Readings – Logistic Regression
To study more about linear regression, please check these links: 1. https://bit.ly/3mjFV76 2. https://bit.ly/2FvcU7B

7.3. KNN Classifier

As discussed in section 6.3, KNN stands for K-nearest neighbors. KNN is a lazy learning algorithm, which is based on finding Euclidean distance between different data points.

The pros and cons of the KNN classifier algorithm are the same as the KNN regression algorithm, which is explained already in Chapter 6, section 6.3.

KNN algorithm can be used both for classification and regression. With Sklearn, it is extremely easy to implement KNN classification. To do so, you can use the KNeighborsClassifier-sclass.

The process of training and testing is the same as linear regression. For training, you need to call the fit() method, and for testing, you need to call the predict() method.

The following script shows the process of training, testing, and evaluating the KNN classification algorithm for predicting the values for the tip column from the Tips dataset.

Script 16:

```
1.  from sklearn.neighbors import KNeighborsClassifier
2.  knn_clf = KNeighborsClassifier(n_neighbors=5)
3.  classifier = knn_clf.fit(X_train, y_train)
4.
5.  y_pred = classifier.predict(X_test)
6.
7.
8.  from sklearn.metrics import classification_
    report, confusion_matrix, accuracy_score
9.
10. print(confusion_matrix(y_test,y_pred))
11. print(classification_report(y_test,y_pred))
12. print(accuracy_score(y_test, y_pred))
```

Output:

```
[[1486  109]
 [ 237  168]]
              precision    recall  f1-score   support

           0       0.86      0.93      0.90      1595
           1       0.61      0.41      0.49       405

    accuracy                           0.83      2000
   macro avg       0.73      0.67      0.69      2000
weighted avg       0.81      0.83      0.81      2000

0.827
```

Further Readings – KNN Classification

To study more about KNN classification, please check these links:

1. https://bit.ly/33pXWlj
2. https://bit.ly/2FqNmZx

7.4. Random Forest Classifier

Like the random forest regressor, the random forest classifier is a tree-based algorithm that converts features into tree nodes, and then uses entropy loss to make classification predictions.

The pros and cons of the random forest classifier algorithm are the same as the random forest regression algorithm, which is explained already in Chapter 6, section 6.4.

RandomForestClassifier class from the Sklearn.ensemble module can be used to implement the random forest regressor algorithm in Python, as shown below.

Script 17:

```
1.  from sklearn.ensemble import RandomForestClassifier
2.  rf_clf = RandomForestClassifier(random_state=42, n_
    estimators=500)
3.
4.  classifier = rf_clf.fit(X_train, y_train)
5.
6.  y_pred = classifier.predict(X_test)
7.
8.
9.  from sklearn.metrics import classification_
    report, confusion_matrix, accuracy_score
10.
11. print(confusion_matrix(y_test,y_pred))
12. print(classification_report(y_test,y_pred))
13. print(accuracy_score(y_test, y_pred))
```

Output:

```
[[1521   74]
 [ 196  209]]
              precision    recall  f1-score   support

           0       0.89      0.95      0.92      1595
           1       0.74      0.52      0.61       405

    accuracy                           0.86      2000
   macro avg       0.81      0.73      0.76      2000
weighted avg       0.86      0.86      0.86      2000

0.865
```

Further Readings - Random Forest Classification

To study more about random forest classification, please check these links:

1. https://bit.ly/2V1GOkO
2. https://bit.ly/2GTyqDH

7.5. Support Vector Classification

The support vector machine is classification as well as regression algorithms, which minimizes the error between the actual predictions and predicted predictions by maximizing the distance between hyperplanes that contain data for various records.

The pros and cons of the support vector classifier algorithm are the same as for the support vector regression algorithm, which is explained already in chapter 6, section 6.5.

With the Sklearn library, you can use the SVM module to implement the support vector classification algorithm, as shown below. The SVC class from the SVM module is used to implement the support vector classification, as shown below:

Script 18:

```
1.  # training SVM algorithm
2.  from sklearn import svm
3.  svm_clf = svm.SVC()
4.
5.  classifier = svm_clf .fit(X_train, y_train)
6.  # making predictions on test set
7.  y_pred = classifier.predict(X_test)
8.
# evaluating algorithm
9.  from sklearn.metrics import classification_
    report, confusion_matrix, accuracy_score
10.
11. print(confusion_matrix(y_test,y_pred))
12. print(classification_report(y_test,y_pred))
13. print(accuracy_score(y_test, y_pred))
```

Output:

```
[[1547    48]
 [ 225  180]]
              precision    recall  f1-score   support

           0       0.87      0.97      0.92      1595
           1       0.79      0.44      0.57       405

    accuracy                           0.86      2000
   macro avg       0.83      0.71      0.74      2000
weighted avg       0.86      0.86      0.85      2000

0.8635
```

Further Readings – SVM Classification

To study more about SVM classification, please check these links:

1. https://bit.ly/3hr4jAi
2. https://bit.ly/3iFOgln

7.6. K-Fold Cross-Validation

You can also perform K-fold cross-validation for classification models, just like regression models. You can use cross_val_score() function from the sklearn.model_selection module to perform cross- validation, as shown below. For the classification algorithm, you need to pass a classification metric, e.g., accuracy to the scoring attribute.

Script 19:

```
1.  from sklearn.model_selection import cross_val_score
2.
3.  print(cross_val_score(classifier, X, y, cv=5,
    scoring ="accuracy"))
```

Output:

```
[0.796  0.796  0.7965 0.7965 0.7965]
```

7.7. Predicting a Single Value

Let's make a prediction on a single customer record and see if he will leave the bank after six months or not.

The following script prints details of the 100th record.

Script 20:

```
1.      churn_df.loc[100]
```

Output:

```
CreditScore              665
Geography             France
Gender                Female
Age                       40
Tenure                     6
Balance                    0
NumOfProducts              1
HasCrCard                  1
IsActiveMember             1
EstimatedSalary       161848
Exited                     0
Name: 100, dtype: object
```

The output above shows that the customer did not exit the bank after six months since the value for the Exited attribute is 0. Let's see what our classification model predicts:

Script 21:

```
1.  # training the random forest algorithm
2.  from sklearn.ensemble import RandomForestClassifier
3.  rf_clf = RandomForestClassifier(random_state=42, n_
    estimators=500)
4.
5.  classifier = rf_clf.fit(X_train, y_train)
6.
7.  # scaling single record
8.  single_record = sc.transform (X.values[100].
    reshape(1, -1))
9.
10. #making predictions on the single record
11. predicted_churn = classifier.predict(single_record)
12. print(predicted_churn)
```

The output is O, which shows that our model correctly predicted that the customer will not churn after six months.

Output:

```
[0]
```

Hands-on Time – Exercise

Now, it is your turn. Follow the instructions in **the exercises below** to check your understanding of the about classification algorithms in machine learning. The answers to these exercises are provided after chapter 10 in this book.

Exercise 7.1

Question 1

Among the following, which one is not an example of classification outputs?

A. True

B. Red

C. Male

D. None of the above

Question 2

Which of the following metrics is used for unbalanced classification datasets?

A. Accuracy

B. F1

C. Precision

D. Recall

Question 3

Among the following functions, which one is used to convert categorical values to one-hot encoded numerical values?

A. pd.get_onehot()

B. pd.get_dummies()

C. pd.get_numeric()

D. All of the above

Exercise 7.2

Using the `iris` dataset from the Seaborn library, train a classification algorithm of your choice, which predicts the species of the iris plant. Perform all the preprocessing steps.

Data Clustering with Machine Learning Using Sklearn Library

In chapters 6 and 7, you studied how to solve regression and classification problems, respectively, using machine learning algorithms in Sklearn. Regression and Classification are types of supervised machine learning problems. In this chapter, you are going to study data clustering algorithms.

Clustering algorithms are unsupervised algorithms where the training data is not labeled. Rather, the algorithms cluster or group the data sets based on common characteristics. In this chapter, you will study two of the most common types of clustering algorithms, i.e., KMeans Clustering and Hierarchical Clustering. You will see how Python's Sklearn library can be used to implement the two clustering algorithms. So, let's begin without much ado.

8.1. K Means Clustering

K Means clustering is one of the most commonly used algorithms for clustering unlabeled data. In K Means clustering, K refers to the number of clusters that you want your data to be grouped into. In K Means clustering, the number of clusters has to be defined before K clustering can be applied to the data points.

Steps for K Means Clustering

The following are the steps that are needed to be performed in order to perform K Means clustering of data points.

1. Randomly assign centroid values for each cluster.

2. Calculate the distance (Euclidean or Manhattan) between each data point and centroid values of all the clusters.

3. Assign the data point to the cluster of the centroid with the shorted distance.

4. Calculate and update centroid values based on the mean values of the coordinates of all the data points of the corresponding cluster.

5. Repeat steps 2-4 until new centroid values for all the clusters are different from the previous centroid values.

Why use K Means Clustering?

K Means clustering is particularly useful when:

1. K Means clustering is a simple to implement algorithm

2. Can be applied to large datasets

3. Scales well to unseen data points

4. Generalize well to clusters of various sizes and shapes.

Disadvantages of K Means Clustering Algorithm

The following are some of the disadvantages of K Means clustering algorithm:

1. The value of K has to be chosen manually

2. Convergence or training time depends on the initial value of K

3. Clustering performance is affected greatly by outliers.

Enough of theory. Let's see how to perform K Means clustering with Scikit learn.

8.1.1. Clustering Dummy Data with Sklearn

Importing the libraries needed is the first step, as shown in the following script:

Script 1:

```
1.  import numpy as np
2.  import pandas as pd
3.  from sklearn.datasets.samples_generator import make_blobs
4.  from sklearn.cluster import KMeans
5.  from matplotlib import pyplot as plt
6.  %matplotlib inline
```

Next, we create a dummy dataset containing 500 records and 4 cluster centers. The average standard deviation between the records is 2.0.

The following script creates a dummy dataset and plots data points on a plot.

Script 2:

```
1. # generating dummy data of 500 records with 4 clusters
2. features, labels = make_blobs(n_samples=500, centers=4,
   cluster_std = 2.00)
3.
4. #plotting the dummy data
5. plt.scatter(features[:,0], features[:,1] )
```

The output looks like this. Using K Means clustering, you will see how we will create four clusters in this dataset.

Output:

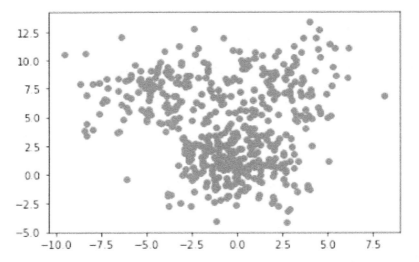

Note:

It is important to mention that dummy data is generated randomly, and hence, you can have a slightly different plot than the plot in the above figure.

To implement K Means clustering, you can use the KMeans class from the sklearn.cluster module. You have to pass the number of clusters as an attribute to the KMeans class constructor. To train the KMeans model, simply pass the dataset to the fit() method of the K Means class, as shown below.

Script 3:

```
1. # performing kmeans clustering using KMeans class
2. km_model = KMeans(n_clusters=4)
3. km_model.fit(features)
```

Once the model is trained, you can print the cluster centers using the cluster_centers_ attribute of the KMeans class object.

Script 4:

```
1. #printing centroid values
2. print(km_model.cluster_centers_)
```

The four cluster centers as predicted by our K Means model has the following coordiantes:

Output:

```
[[-4.54070231  7.26625699]
 [ 0.10118215 -0.23788283]
 [ 2.57107155  8.17934929]
 [-0.38501161  3.11446039]]
```

In addition to finding cluster centers, the KMeans class also assigns a cluster label to each data point. The cluster labels are numbers that basically serve as cluster id. For instance, in the case of four clusters, the cluster ids are 0,1,2,3.

To print the cluster ids for all the labels, you can use the labels_ attribute of the KMeans class, as shown below.

Script 5:

```
1. #printing predicted label values
2. print(km_model.labels_)
```

Output:

```
[0 2 3 2 1 1 3 1 2 0 0 2 3 3 1 1 2 0 1 2 2 1 3 3 1 1 0 2 0 2 0
 1 0 1 3 2 2 3 0 0 0 2 1 2 0 1 3 1 3 2 1 3 3 1 0 2 1 3 0 0 3 3
 3 1 1 1 3 0 1 3 2 1 1 2 0 2 1 2 1 0 0 2 1 2 1 0 2 0 0 2 2 3 3
 0 2 0 2 3 0 0 3 1 0 3 2 1 3 2 2 0 2 1 1 0 0 3 3 2 3 1 0 0 3 0
 1 0 3 1 0 3 2 0 1 1 0 2 1 2 2 0 3 1 3 3 0 1 1 0 2 0 0 0 3 3 3
 3 0 3 1 2 1 0 3 2 3 1 3 3 0 3 2 3 0 1 3 2 3 2 1 2 2 3 0 3 2 0
 3 0 1 2 2 3 2 2 1 0 1 1 2 3 2 0 1 3 3 3 3 0 0 3 1 0 1 1 3 3 1
 3 1 0 0 2 1 1 1 1 2 2 0 2 1 0 1 2 3 0 1 2 0 1 1 0 1 0 3 1 2 1
 1 2 3 0 0 1 3 1 2 0 1 1 0 1 0 0 2 2 0 1 2 0 1 2 0 0 1 1 0 1 2
 3 0 1 2 3 0 0 3 2 3 0 3 1 3 1 3 0 1 3 3 1 1 2 2 2 3 1 1 3 1 3
 3 0 1 1 2 0 2 2 3 1 0 3 2 1 0 2 3 1 0 2 0 0 3 1 1 2 3 3 1 2 2
 3 0 3 3 3 1 0 2 0 0 3 1 1 0 1 0 3 1 3 1 0 0 1 3 1 2 0 0 0 1 1
 0 0 2 0 0 2 2 3 2 3 3 3 0 3 1 1 1 1 3 1 1 1 2 3 0 2 3 3 1 1 3
 3 3 3 3 0 0 3 2 0 3 2 1 1 3 2 1 2 1 1 1 3 3 2 3 1 1 1 2 0 2 1
 1 0 0 3 1 2 3 0 2 0 2 0 2 3 3 2 2 0 0 2 0 0 0 1 3 2 2 1 1 2 1
 1 0 1 2 1 0 0 2 2 0 3 3 0 0 2 1 3 2 0 3 3 1 2 1 1 3 0 3 3 0 0
 1 2 3 1]
```

The following script prints the clusters in different colors along with the cluster centers as black data points, as shown below.

Script 6:

```
1.  #pring the data points
2.  plt.scatter(features[:,0], features[:,1], c= km_model.
    labels_, cmap='rainbow' )
3.
4.  #print the centroids
5.  plt.scatter(km_model.cluster_centers_[:, 0], km_model.
    cluster_centers_[:, 1], s=100, c='black')
```

The following output shows the four clusters identified by the K Means clustering algorithm.

Output:

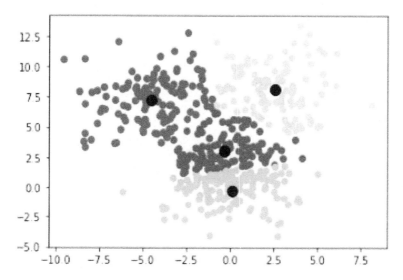

The following script prints the actual four clusters in the dataset.

Script 7:

```
1. #print actual datapoints
2. plt.scatter(features[:,0], features[:,1], c= labels,
   cmap='rainbow' )
```

The output shows that in the actual dataset, the clusters represented by red and yellow data points overlap. However, the predicted clusters do not contain any overlapping data points.

Output:

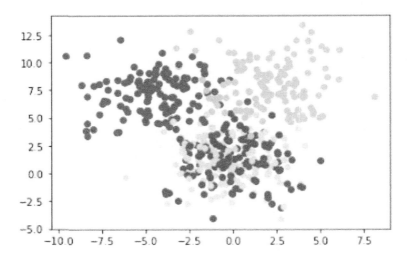

Note:

The color of the clusters doesn't have to be the same since cluster colors are randomly generated at runtime—only the cluster positions matter.

8.1.2. Clustering Iris Dataset

In the previous section, you saw a clustering example of some dummy dataset. In this section, we will cluster the Iris dataset. The Iris dataset can be imported via the following script.

Script 8:

```
1. import seaborn as sns
2.
3. iris_df = sns.load_dataset("iris")
4. iris_df.head()
```

Output:

	sepal_length	sepal_width	petal_length	petal_width	species
0	5.1	3.5	1.4	0.2	setosa
1	4.9	3.0	1.4	0.2	setosa
2	4.7	3.2	1.3	0.2	setosa
3	4.6	3.1	1.5	0.2	setosa
4	5.0	3.6	1.4	0.2	setosa

We do not use data labels for clustering. Hence, we will separate features from labels. Execute the following script to do so:

Script 9:

```
1.  # dividing data into features and labels
2.  features = iris_df.drop(["species"], axis = 1)
3.  labels = iris_df.filter(["species"], axis = 1)
4.  features.head()
```

Here is the feature set we want to cluster.

Output:

	sepal_length	sepal_width	petal_length	petal_width
0	5.1	3.5	1.4	0.2
1	4.9	3.0	1.4	0.2
2	4.7	3.2	1.3	0.2
3	4.6	3.1	1.5	0.2
4	5.0	3.6	1.4	0.2

Let's first choose 4 as a random number for the number of clusters. The following script performs K Means clustering on the Iris dataset.

Script 10:

```
1.  # training KMeans model
2.  features = features.values
3.  km_model = KMeans(n_clusters=4)
4.  km_model.fit(features)
```

To print labels of the Iris dataset, execute the following script:

Script 11:

```
1.  print(km_model.labels_)
```

Output:

```
[1 1 1 1 1 1 1 1 1 1 1 1 1 1 1 1 1 1 1 1 1 1 1 1 1 1 1 1 1 1
 1 1 1 1 1 1 1 1 1 1 1 1 1 1 1 1 1 1 1 1 2 2 2 3 2 3 2 3 2 3 3 3
 3 2 3 2 3 3 3 2 3 2 3 2 2 2 2 2 2 2 3 3 3 3 2 3 2 3 2 2 2 3 3 3 2 3
 3 3 3 3 2 3 3 0 2 0 0 0 0 3 0 0 0 2 2 0 2 2 0 0 0 0 2 0 2 0 2
 0 0 2 2 0 0 0 0 0 2 2 0 0 0 2 0 0 0 2 0 0 0 2 2 0 2]
```

Finally, to plot the 4 clusters found by the K Means algorithm in the Iris dataset, along with the predicted cluster centroids, execute the following script.

Script 12:

```
1.  #pring the data points
2.  plt.scatter(features[:,0], features[:,1], c= km_model.
    labels_, cmap='rainbow' )
3.
4.  #print the centroids
5.  plt.scatter(km_model.cluster_centers_[:, 0], km_model.
    cluster_centers_[:, 1], s=100, c='black')
```

Output:

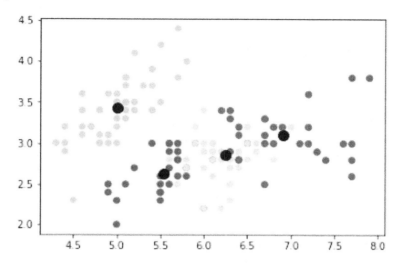

Till now, in this chapter, we have been randomly initializing the value of K or the number of clusters. However, there is a way to find the ideal number of clusters. The method is known as the elbow method. In the elbow method, the value of inertia obtained by training K Means clusters with different number of K is plotted.

The inertia represents the total distance between the data points within a cluster. Smaller inertia means that the predicted clusters are robust and close to the actual clusters.

To calculate the inertia value, you can use the inertia_ attribute of the KMeans class object. The following script creates inertial values for K=1 to 10 and plots in the form of a line plot, as shown below:

Script 13:

```
1.  # training KMeans on K values from 1 to 10
2.  loss =[]
3.  for i in range(1, 11):
4.      km = KMeans(n_clusters = i).fit(features)
5.      loss.append(km.inertia_)
6.
7.  #printing loss against number of clusters
8.
9.  import matplotlib.pyplot as plt
10. plt.plot(range(1, 11), loss)
11. plt.title('Finding Optimal Clusters via Elbow Method')
12. plt.xlabel('Number of Clusters')
13. plt.ylabel('loss')
14. plt.show()
```

From the output below, it can be seen that the value of inertia didn't decrease much after 3 clusters.

Output:

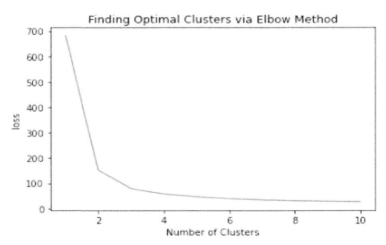

Let's now cluster the Iris data using 3 clusters and see if we can get close to the actual clusters.

Script 14:

```
1.  # training KMeans with 3 clusters
2.  km_model = KMeans(n_clusters=3)
3.  km_model.fit(features)
```

Script 15:

```
1.  #pring the data points with prediced labels
2.  plt.scatter(features[:,0], features[:,1], c= km_model.
    labels_, cmap='rainbow' )
3.
4.  #print the predicted centroids
5.  plt.scatter(km_model.cluster_centers_[:, 0], km_model.
    cluster_centers_[:, 1], s=100, c='black')
```

When K is 3, the number of clusters predicted by the K Means clustering algorithm is as follows:

Output:

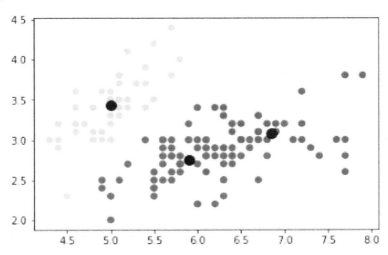

Let's now plot the actual clusters and see how close the actual clusters are to predicted clusters.

Script 16:

```
1. # converting categorical labels to numbers
2.
3. from sklearn import preprocessing
4. le = preprocessing.LabelEncoder()
5. labels = le.fit_transform(labels)
6.
7. #pring the data points with original labels
8. plt.scatter(features[:,0], features[:,1], c= labels,
   cmap='rainbow' )
```

The output shows that the actual clusters are pretty close to predicted clusters.

Output:

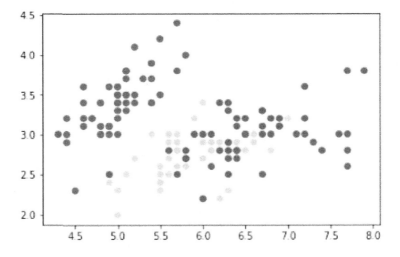

8.2. Hierarchical Clustering

Like K Means clustering, hierarchical clustering is another commonly used unsupervised machine learning technique for data clustering.

Hierarchical clustering can be broadly divided into two types: agglomerative clustering and divisive clustering. Agglomerative clustering follows a bottom-up approach, where individual data points are clustered together to form multiple small clusters leading to a big cluster, which can then be divided into small clusters using dendrograms. On the other hand, in the case of divisive clustering, you have one big cluster, which you divide into N number of small clusters.

In this chapter, you will perform agglomerative clustering using the Sklearn library.

Steps for Hierarchical Agglomerative Clustering

The steps required to perform agglomerative clustering are as follows:

1. Consider each data point in the dataset as one cluster. Hence, the number of clusters in the beginning is equal to the number of data points.

2. Join the two closest data points to form a cluster.

3. Form more clusters by joining the closest clusters. Repeat this process until one big cluster is formed.

4. Use dendrograms to divide the one big cluster into multiple small clusters. (The concept of dendrograms is explained later in the chapter.)

Why Use Hierarchical Clustering?

Hierarchical clustering has the following advantages:

1. Unlike K Means clustering, for hierarchical clustering, you do not have to specify the number of centroids clustering.

2. With dendrograms, it is easier to interpret how data has been clustered.

Disadvantages of Hierarchical Clustering Algorithm

The following are some of the disadvantages of the hierarchical clustering algorithm:

1. Doesn't scale well on unseen data.

2. Has higher time complexity compared to K Means clustering.

3. Difficult to determine the number of clusters in case of a large dataset.

In the next section, you will see how to perform agglomerative clustering via Sklearn.

8.2.1. Clustering Dummy Data

First, we will see how to perform hierarchical clustering on dummy data, and then we will perform hierarchical clustering on Iris data.

Example 1

In the first example, we will perform agglomerative clustering of 10 2-dimensional data points only.

The following script imports the required libraries:

Script 17:

```
1. import numpy as np
2. import pandas as pd
3. from sklearn.datasets.samples_generator import make_blobs
4. from matplotlib import pyplot as plt
5. %matplotlib inline
```

The following script randomly creates data points and then labels the data points from 1 to 10. The data points are plotted as a scatter plot.

Script 18:

```
1.  # generating dummy data of 10 records with 2 clusters
2.  features, labels = make_blobs(n_samples=10, centers=2,
    cluster_std = 2.00)
3.
4.  #plotting the dummy data
5.  plt.scatter(features[:,0], features[:,1], color ='r' )
6.
7.  #adding numbers to data points
8.  annots = range(1, 11)
9.  for label, x, y  in zip(annots, features[:, 0],
    features[:, 1]):
10.     plt.annotate(
11.         label,
12.         xy=(x, y), xytext=(-3, 3),
13.         textcoords='offset points', ha='right', va='bottom')
14. plt.show()
```

The output is as follows. From the output below, it can be clearly seen that the data points 1, 2, 3, 5, and 10 belong to one cluster and the data points 4, 6, 7, 8, and 9 belong to the other cluster.

Output:

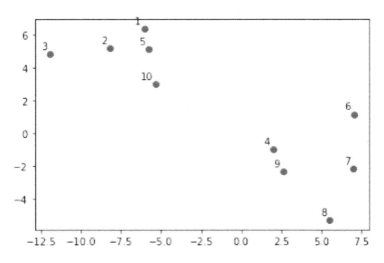

Let's now plot dendrograms for the above 10 data points. To plot dendrograms, you can use the dendrogram and linkage classes from the scipy.cluster.hierarchy module. The features are passed to the linkage class. And the object of the linkage class is passed to the dendrogram class to plot dendrogram for the features, as shown in the following script:

Script 19:

```
1.  from scipy.cluster.hierarchy import dendrogram, linkage
2.
3.
4.  dendos = linkage(features, 'single')
5.
6.  annots = range(1, 11)
7.
8.  dendrogram(dendos,
9.                 orientation='top',
10.                labels=annots,
11.                distance_sort='descending',
12.                show_leaf_counts=True)
13. plt.show()
```

Here is the output of the above script.

Output:

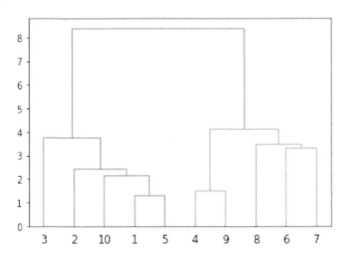

From the figure above, it can be seen that points 1 and 5 are closest to each other. Hence, a cluster is formed by connecting these points. The cluster of 1 and 5 is closest to data point 10, resulting in a cluster containing points 1, 5, and 10. In the same way, the remaining clusters are formed until a big cluster is formed.

After a big cluster is formed, select the longest vertical line. Then, draw a horizontal line through it. The number of clusters formed is equal to the number of vertical lines this newly created horizontal line passes.

For instance, in the following figure, two clusters are formed.

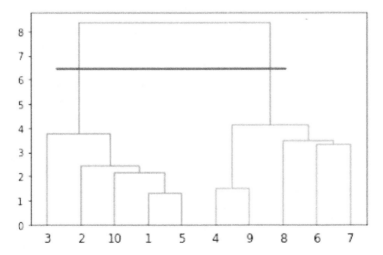

In real world scenarios, there can be thousands of data points, and hence, the dendrogram method cannot be used to manually cluster the data. This is where we can use the AgglomerativeClustering class from the sklearn.cluster module. The number of clusters and the distance types are passed as parameters to the AgglomerativeClustering class.

The following script applies agglomerative clustering to our dummy dataset.

Script 20:

```
1.  from sklearn.cluster import AgglomerativeClustering
2.
3.  # training agglomerative clustering model
4.  hc_model = AgglomerativeClustering(n_
    clusters=2, affinity='euclidean', linkage='ward')
5.  hc_model.fit_predict(features)
```

Output:

```
array([0, 0, 0, 1, 0, 1, 1, 1, 1, 0], dtype=int64)
```

And the following script plots the predicted clusters.

Script 21:

```
1.  #pring the data points
2.  plt.scatter(features[:,0], features[:,1], c= hc_model.
    labels_, cmap='rainbow' )
```

The output shows that our clustering algorithm has successfully clustered the data points.

Output:

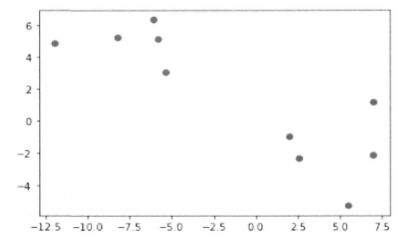

Example 2

In the previous example, we had 10 data points with 2 clusters. Let's now see an example with 500 data points. The following script creates 500 data points with 4 cluster centers.

Script 22:

```
1.  # generating dummy data of 500 records with 4 clusters
2.  features, labels = make_blobs(n_
    samples=500, centers=4, cluster_std = 2.00)
3.
4.  #plotting the dummy data
5.  plt.scatter(features[:,0], features[:,1] )
```

Output:

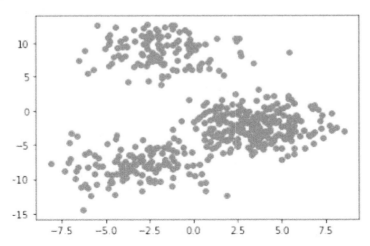

The following script applies agglomerative hierarchical clustering on the dataset. The number of predicted clusters is 4.

Script 23:

```
1.  # performing kmeans clustering using
    AgglomerativeClustering class
2.  hc_model = AgglomerativeClustering(n_clusters=4, affinity=
    'euclidean', linkage='ward')
3.  hc_model.fit_predict(features)
```

The output shows the labels of some of the data points in our dataset. You can see that since there are 4 clusters, there are 4 unique labels, i.e., 0, 1, 2, and 3.

Output:

```
array([0, 1, 1, 0, 1, 0, 3, 0, 0, 1, 0, 0, 1, 3, 0, 2, 0, 3,
1, 0, 0, 0,], dtype=int64)
```

To plot the predicted clusters, execute the following script.

Script 24:

```
1.  #pring the data points
2.  plt.scatter(features[:,0], features[:,1], c= hc_model.
    labels_, cmap='rainbow' )
```

Output:

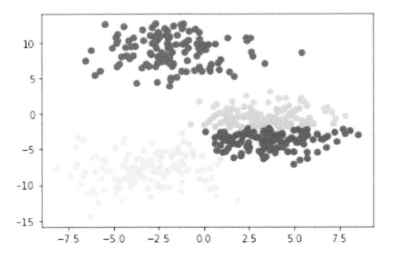

Similarly, to plot the actual clusters in the dataset (for the sake of comparison), execute the following script.

Script 25:

```
1.  #print actual datapoints
2.  plt.scatter(features[:,0], features[:,1], c= labels,
    cmap='rainbow' )
```

Output:

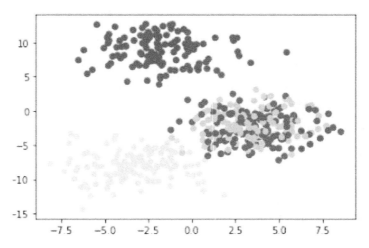

8.2.2. Clustering the Iris Dataset

In this section, you will see how to cluster the Iris dataset using hierarchical agglomerative clustering. The following script imports the Iris dataset and displays the first five rows of the dataset.

Script 26:

```
1.  import seaborn as sns
2.
3.  iris_df = sns.load_dataset("iris")
4.  iris_df.head()
```

Output:

	sepal_length	sepal_width	petal_length	petal_width	species
0	5.1	3.5	1.4	0.2	setosa
1	4.9	3.0	1.4	0.2	setosa
2	4.7	3.2	1.3	0.2	setosa
3	4.6	3.1	1.5	0.2	setosa
4	5.0	3.6	1.4	0.2	setosa

The following script divides the data into features and labels sets and displays the first five rows of the labels set.

Script 27:

```
1.  # dividing data into features and labels
2.  features = iris_df.drop(["species"], axis = 1)
3.  labels = iris_df.filter(["species"], axis = 1)
4.  features.head()
```

Output:

	sepal_length	sepal_width	petal_length	petal_width
0	5.1	3.5	1.4	0.2
1	4.9	3.0	1.4	0.2
2	4.7	3.2	1.3	0.2
3	4.6	3.1	1.5	0.2
4	5.0	3.6	1.4	0.2

Similarly, the following script applies the agglomerative clustering on the feature set using the AgglomerativeClustering class from the sklearn.cluster module.

Script 28:

```
1.  # training Hierarchical clustering model
2.  from sklearn.cluster import AgglomerativeClustering
3.
4.  # training agglomerative clustering model
5.  features = features.values
6.  hc_model = AgglomerativeClustering(n_
    clusters=3, affinity='euclidean', linkage='ward')
7.  hc_model.fit_predict(features)
```

The output below shows the predicted cluster labels for the feature set in the Iris dataset.

Output:

```
array([1, 1, 1, 1, 1, 1, 1, 1, 1, 1, 1, 1, 1, 1, 1, 1, 1, 1,
       1, 1, 1, 1, 1, 1, 1, 1, 1, 1, 1, 1, 1, 1, 1, 1, 1, 1,
       1, 1, 1, 1, 1, 1, 1, 1, 1, 1, 1, 1, 1, 1, 0, 0, 0, 0,
       0, 0, 0, 0, 0, 0, 0, 0, 0, 0, 0, 0, 0, 0, 0, 0, 0, 0,
       0, 0, 0, 0, 0, 2, 0, 0, 0, 0, 0, 0, 0, 0, 0, 0, 0, 0,
       0, 0, 0, 0, 0, 0, 0, 0, 0, 0, 2, 0, 2, 2, 2, 2, 0, 2,
       2, 2, 2, 2, 2, 0, 0, 2, 2, 2, 2, 0, 2, 0, 2, 0, 2, 2,
       0, 0, 2, 2, 2, 2, 2, 0, 0, 2, 2, 2, 0, 2, 2, 2, 0, 2,
       2, 2, 0, 2, 2, 0], dtype=int64)
```

The predicted clusters are printed via the following script.

Script 29:

```
1.  #pring the data points
2.  plt.scatter(features[:,0], features[:,1], c= hc_model.
    labels_, cmap='rainbow' )
```

Output:

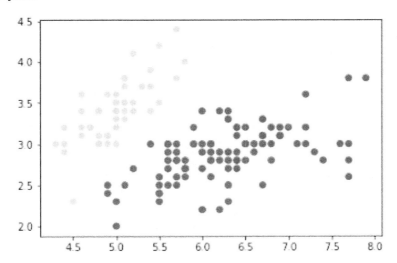

You can also create dendrograms using the feature set using the shc module from the scipy.cluster.hierarchy library. You have to pass the feature set to the linkage class of the shc module, and then the object of the linkage class is passed to the dendrogram class to plot the dendrograms, as shown in the following script.

Script 30:

```
1.  import scipy.cluster.hierarchy as shc
2.
3.  plt.figure(figsize=(10, 7))
4.  plt.title("Iris Dendograms")
5.  dend = shc.dendrogram(shc.linkage(features, method='ward'))
```

Here is the output of the script above.

Output:

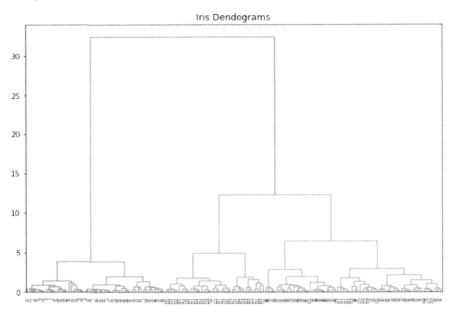

If you want to cluster the dataset into three clusters, you can simply draw a horizontal line that passes through the three vertical lines, as shown below. The clusters below the horizontal line are the resultant clusters. In the following figure, we form three clusters.

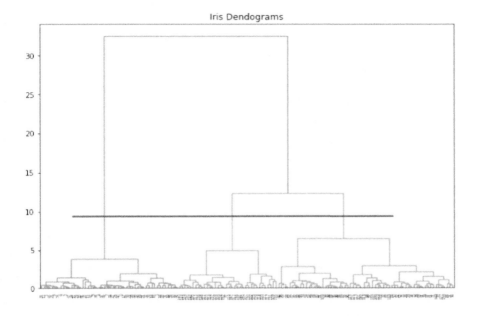

Exercise 8.1

Question 1

Which of the following is a supervised machine learning algorithm?

    A. K Means Clustering

    B. Hierarchical Clustering

    C. All of the above

    D. None of the above

Question 2

In KMeans clustering, what does the inertia tell us?

    A. the distance between data points within cluster

    B. output labels for the data points

    C. the number of clusters

    D. None of the above

Question 3

In hierarchical clustering, in the case of vertical dendrograms, the number of clusters is equal to the number of _____ lines that the _____ line passes through?

    A. horizontal, vertical

    B. vertical, horizontal

    C. none of the above

    D. All of the above

Exercise 8.2

Apply KMeans clustering on the banknote.csv dataset available in the *Datasets* folder in the GitHub repository. Find the optimal number of clusters and then print the clustered dataset. The following script imports the dataset and prints the first five rows of the dataset.

Deep Learning with Python TensorFlow 2.0

In this chapter, you will be using TensorFlow 2.0 and Keras API to implement different types of neural networks in Python. From TensorFlow 2.0, Google has officially adopted Keras as the main API to run TensorFlow scripts.

In this chapter, you will study three different types of Neural Networks: Densely Connected Neural Network, Recurrent Neural Network, and Convolutional Neural Network, with TensorFlow 2.0.

9.1. Densely Connected Neural Network

A densely connected neural network (DNN) is a type of neural network where all the nodes in the previous layer are connected to all the nodes in the subsequent layer of a neural network. A DNN is also called a multilayer perceptron.

A densely connected neural network is mostly used for making predictions on tabular data. Tabular data is the type of data that can be presented in the form of a table.

In a neural network, we have an input layer, one or multiple hidden layers, and an output layer. An example of a neural network is shown below:

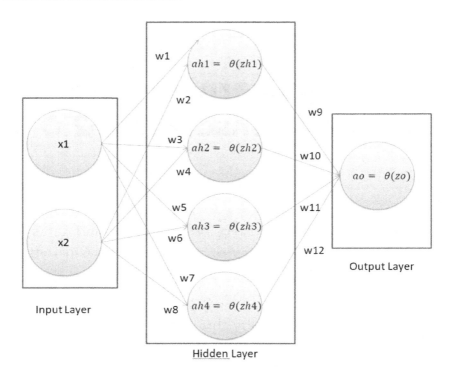

In our neural network, we have two nodes in the input layer (since there are two features in the input), one hidden layer with four nodes, and one output layer with one node since we are doing binary classification. The number of hidden layers, along with the number of neurons per hidden layer, depends upon you.

In the above neural network, the x1 and x2 are the input features, and the ao is the output of the network. Here, the only attribute we can control is the weights w1, w2, w3, ... w12. The idea is to find the values of weights for which the difference between the predicted output ao in this case and the actual output (labels).

A neural network works in two steps:

1. Feed Forward
2. Backpropagation

I will explain both these steps in the context of our neural network.

9.1.1. Feed Forward

In the feed forward step, the final output of a neural network is created. Let's try to find the final output of our neural network.

In our neural network, we will first find the value of zh1, which can be calculated as follows:

$$zh_1 = x_1 \times w_1 + x_2 \times w_2 + b \text{---------- (1)}$$

Using zh1, we can find the value of ah1, which is:

$$ah_1 = \frac{1}{\left(1 + e^{-zh_1}\right)} \text{---------- (2)}$$

In the same way, you find the values of ah2, ah3, and ah4.

To find the value of zo, you can use the following formula:

$$zo = ah_1 \times w_9 + ah_2 \times w_{10} + ah_3 \times w_{11} + ah_4 \times w_{12} \text{---- (3)}$$

Finally, to find the output of the neural network ao:

$$ao = \frac{1}{\left(1 + e^{-zo}\right)} \text{---------- (4)}$$

9.1.2. Backpropagation

The purpose of backpropagation is to minimize the overall loss by finding the optimum values of weights. The loss function we are going to use in this section is the mean squared error, which is in our case represented as:

$$J = \frac{1}{m} \sum_{i=1}^{m} (ao_i - y_i)^2$$

Here, ao is the predicted output from our neural network, and y is the actual output.

Our weights are divided into two parts. We have weights that connect input features to the hidden layer and the hidden layer to the output node. We call the weights that connect the input to the hidden layer collectively as wh (w1, w2, w3 ...... w8), and the weights connecting the hidden layer to the output as wo (w9, w10, w11, w12).

The backpropagation will consist of two phases. In the first phase, we will find dcost/dwo (which refers to the derivative of the total cost with respect to wo, weights in the output layer). By the chain rule, dcost/dwo can be represented as the product of dcost/dao * dao/dzo * dzo/dwo. (d here refers to a derivative.) Mathematically:

$$\frac{dcost}{dwo} = \left(\frac{dcost}{dao}\right) \times \left(\frac{dao}{dzo}\right) \times \left(\frac{dzo}{dwo}\right) \text{------ (5)}$$

$$\frac{dcost}{dao} = \frac{1}{m}(ao - y) \text{------- (6)}$$

$$\frac{dao}{dzo} = sigmoid(zo) \times (1 - sigmoid(zo)) \text{--- (7)}$$

$$\frac{dzo}{dwo}=ah.T$$
----- (8)

In the same way, you find the derivative of cost with respect to bias in the output layer, i.e., dcost/dbo, which is given as:

$$\frac{dcost}{dbo}=\left(\frac{dcost}{dao}\right)\times\left(\frac{dao}{dzo}\right)$$

Putting 6, 7, and 8 in equation 5, we can get the derivative of cost with respect to the output weights.

The next step is to find the derivative of cost with respect to hidden layer weights wh and bias bh. Let's first find the derivative of cost with respect to hidden layer weights:

$$\frac{dcost}{dwh}=\left(\frac{dcost}{dah}\right)\times\left(\frac{dah}{dzh}\right)\times\left(\frac{dzh}{dwh}\right)$$
..... (9)

$$\frac{dcost}{dah}=\left(\frac{dcost}{dao}\right)\times\left(\frac{dao}{dzo}\right)\times\left(\frac{dzo}{dah}\right)$$
.... (10)

The values of dcost/dao and dao/dzo can be calculated from equations 6 and 7, respectively. The value of dzo/dah is given as:

$$\frac{dzo}{dah}=wo.T$$
...... (11)

Putting the values of equations 6, 7, and 11 in equation 11, you can get the value of equation 10.

Next, let's find the value of dah/dzh:

$$\frac{dah}{dzh}=sigmoid(zh)\times(1\text{-}sigmoid(zh))$$
..... (12)

and,

$$\frac{dzh}{dwh} = X.T$$
...... (13)

Using equation 10, 12, and 13 in equation 9, you can find the value of dcost/dwh.

9.1.3. Implementing a Densely Connected Neural Network

In this section, you will see how to implement a densely connected neural network with TensorFlow, which predicts whether or not a banknote is genuine or not, based on certain features such as variance, skewness, curtosis, and entropy of several banknote images. Let's begin without much ado. The following script upgrades the existing TensorFlow version. I always recommend doing this.

Script 1:

```
pip install --upgrade tensorflow
```

To check if you are actually running TensorFlow 2.0, execute the following command.

Script 2:

```
1. import tensorflow as tf
2. print(tf.__version__)
```

You should see 2.x.x in the output, as shown below:

Output:

```
2.1.0
```

§ Importing Required Libraries

Let's import the required libraries.

Script 3:

```
1. importseaborn as sns
2. import pandas as pd
3. importnumpy as np
4. fromtensorflow.keras.
   layers import Dense, Dropout, Activation
5. fromtensorflow.keras.models import Model, Sequential
6. fromtensorflow.keras.optimizers import Adam
```

§ Importing the Dataset

The dataset that we are going to use can be downloaded free from the following GitHub resource. The dataset is also available by the name "banknotes.csv" in the *Datasets* folder in the GitHub repository.

Script 4:

```
1. # reading data from CSV File
2. banknote_data = pd.read_csv("https://raw.githubusercontent.
   com/AbhiRoy96/Banknote-Authentication-UCI-Dataset/master/
   bank_notes.csv")
```

The following script plots the first five rows of the dataset.

Script 5:

```
1.    banknote_data.head()
```

Output:

	variance	skewness	curtosis	entropy	Target
0	3.62160	8.6661	-2.8073	-0.44699	0
1	4.54590	8.1674	-2.4586	-1.46210	0
2	3.86600	-2.6383	1.9242	0.10645	0
3	3.45660	9.5228	-4.0112	-3.59440	0
4	0.32924	-4.4552	4.5718	-0.98880	0

The output shows that our dataset contains five columns. Let's see the shape of our dataset.

Script 6:

```
1.  banknote_data.shape
```

The output shows that our dataset has 1372 rows and 5 columns.

Output:

```
(1372, 5)
```

Let's plot a count plot to see the distribution of data with respect to the values in the class that we want to predict.

Script 7:

```
1.  sns.countplot(x='Target', data=banknote_data)
```

Output:

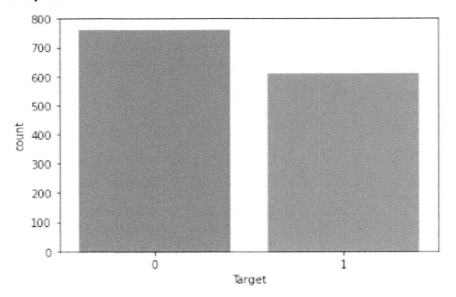

The output shows that the number of fake notes (represented by 1) is slightly less than the number of original banknotes.

The task is to predict the values for the "Target" column, based on the values in the first four columns. Let's divide our data into features and target labels.

Script 8:

```
1.  X = banknote_data.drop(['Target'], axis=1).values
2.  y = banknote_data[['Target']].values
3.
4.  print(X.shape)
5.  print(y.shape)
```

Output:

```
(1372, 4)
(1372, 1)
```

The variable X contains our feature set while the variable y contains target labels.

§ Dividing Data into Training and Test Sets

Deep learning models are normally trained on one set of data and are tested on another set. The dataset used to train a deep learning model is called a training set, and the dataset used to evaluate the performance of the trained deep learning model is called the test set.

We will divide the total data into an 80 percent training set and a 20 percent test set. The following script performs that task.

Script 9:

```
1.  from sklearn.model_selection import train_test_split
2.  X_train, X_test, y_train, y_test = train_test_
    split(X, y, test_size=0.20, random_state=42)
```

Before you train your deep learning model, it is always a good practice to scale your data. The following script applies standard scaling to the training and test sets.

Script 10:

```
1. fromsklearn.preprocessing import StandardScaler
2. sc = StandardScaler()
3. X_train = sc.fit_transform(X_train)
4. X_test = sc.transform(X_test)
```

§ Creating a Neural Network

To create a neural network, you can use the **Sequential** class from the **tensorflow.keras.models** module. To add layers to your model, you simply need to call the add method and pass your layer to it. To create a dense layer, you can use the **Dense** class.

The first parameter to the **Dense** class is the number of nodes in the dense layer, and the second parameter is the dimension of the input. The activation function can be defined by passing a string value to the activation attribute of the Dense class. It is important to mention that the input dimensions are only required to be passed to the first dense layer. The subsequent dense layers can calculate the input dimensions automatically from the number of nodes in the previous layers.

The following script defines a method **create_model**. The model takes two parameters: **learning_rate** and **dropout_rate**. Inside the model, we create an object of the **Sequential** class and add three dense layers to the model. The layers contain 12, 6, and 1 nodes, respectively. After each dense layer, we add a dropout layer with a dropout rate of 0.1. Adding dropout after each layer avoids overfitting. After you create the model, you need to compile it via the compile method. The compile method takes the loss function, the optimizer, and the metrics as parameters. Remember, for binary classification, the activation function in the final dense layer will be **sigmoid**, whereas the loss function in the compile method will be **binary_crossentropy**.

Script 11:

```
def create_model(learning_rate, dropout_rate):

#create sequential model
    model = Sequential()
#adding dense layers
    model.add(Dense(12, input_dim=X_train.
shape[1], activation='relu'))
    model.add(Dropout(dropout_rate))
    model.add(Dense(6, activation='relu'))
    model.add(Dropout(dropout_rate))
    model.add(Dense(1, activation='sigmoid'))
#compiling the model
    adam = Adam(lr=learning_rate)
    model.compile(loss='binary_
crossentropy', optimizer=adam, metrics=['accuracy'])
    return model
```

Next, we need to define the default dropout rate, learning rate batch size, and the number of epochs. The number of epochs refers to the number of times the whole dataset is used for training, and the batch size refers to the number of records, after which the weights are updated.

```
1.  dropout_rate = 0.1
2.  epochs = 20
3.  batch_size = 4
4.  learn_rate = 0.001
```

The following script creates our model.

Script 12:

```
1. model = create_model(learn_rate, dropout_rate)
```

You can see your model architecture via the **plot_model()** method of the **tensorflow.keras.utils** module.

Script 13:

```
1. from tensorflow.keras.utils import plot_model
2. plot_model(model, to_file='model_plot1.png', show_
   shapes=True, show_layer_names=True)
```

Output:

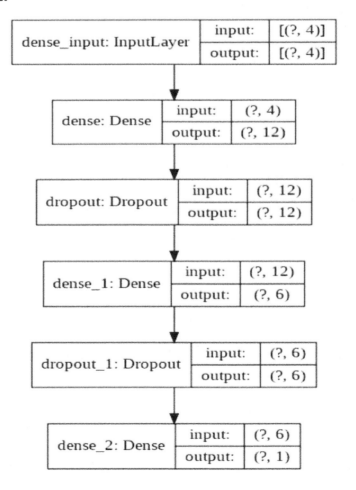

From the above output, you can see that the input layer contains four nodes, the input to the first dense layers is 4, while the output is 12. Similarly, the input to the second dense layer is 12, while the output is 6. Finally, in the last dense layer, the input is 6 nodes, while the output is 1 since we are making a binary classification. Also, you can see a dropout layer after each dense layer.

To train the model, you need to call the fit method on the model object. The fit method takes the training features and targets as parameters, along with the batch size, the number of epochs, and the validation split. The validation split refers to the split in the training data during training.

Script 14:

```
1.  model_history = model.fit(X_train, y_train, batch_
    size=batch_
2.  size, epochs=epochs, validation_split=0.2, verbose=1)
```

The result from the last five epochs is shown below:

Output:

```
Epoch 15/20
877/877 [==============================] - 1s 1ms/sample - loss: 0.0230 - accuracy: 0.9943 - val_loss: 0.0067 - val_accuracy: 1.0000
Epoch 16/20
877/877 [==============================] - 1s 1ms/sample - loss: 0.0209 - accuracy: 0.9954 - val_loss: 0.0051 - val_accuracy: 1.0000
Epoch 17/20
877/877 [==============================] - 1s 1ms/sample - loss: 0.0204 - accuracy: 0.9977 - val_loss: 0.0040 - val_accuracy: 1.0000
Epoch 18/20
877/877 [==============================] - 1s 1ms/sample - loss: 0.0136 - accuracy: 0.9977 - val_loss: 0.0040 - val_accuracy: 1.0000
Epoch 19/20
877/877 [==============================] - 1s 1ms/sample - loss: 0.0234 - accuracy: 0.9954 - val_loss: 0.0047 - val_accuracy: 1.0000
Epoch 20/20
877/877 [==============================] - 1s 1ms/sample - loss: 0.0176 - accuracy: 0.9943 - val_loss: 0.0030 - val_accuracy: 1.0000
```

Our neural network is now trained. The "val_accuracy" of 1.0 in the last epoch shows that on the training set, our neural network is making predictions with 100 percent accuracy.

§ Evaluating the Neural Network Performance

We can now evaluate its performance by making predictions on the test set. To make predictions on the test set, you have to pass the set to the evaluate() method of the model, as shown below:

Script 15:

```
1. accuracies = model.evaluate(X_test, y_test, verbose=1)
2. print("Test Score:", accuracies[0])
3. print("Test Accuracy:", accuracies[1])
```

Output:

```
275/275 [==============================] - 0s 374us/sample -
loss: 0.0040 - accuracy: 1.0000
Test Score: 0.00397354013286531
Test Accuracy: 1.0
```

The output shows an accuracy of 100 percent on the test set. The loss value of 0.00397 is shown. Remember, lower the loss, higher the accuracy.

Let's now plot the accuracy on the training and test sets to see if our model is overfitting or not.

Script 16:

```
1. importmatplotlib.pyplot as plt
2. plt.plot(model_history.
   history['accuracy'], label = 'accuracy')
3. plt.plot(model_history.history['val_
   accuracy'], label = 'val_ accuracy')
4. plt.legend(['train','test'], loc='lowerleft')
```

Output:

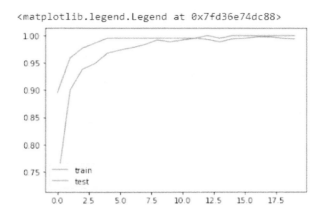

The above curve meets near 1 and then becomes stable which shows that our model is not overfitting.

Similarly, the loss values for test and training sets can be printed as follows:

Script 17:

```
1.  plt.plot(model_history.history['loss'], label = 'loss')
2.  plt.plot(model_history.history['val_loss'], label = 'val_
    loss')
3.  plt.legend(['train','test'], loc='upper left')
```

Output:

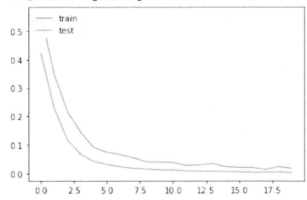

And this is it. You have successfully trained a neural network for classification. In the next section, you will see how to create and train a recurrent neural network for stock price prediction.

9.2. Recurrent Neural Networks (RNN)

9.2.1. What Is an RNN and LSTM?

This section explains what a recurrent neural network (RNN) is, what is the problem with RNN, and how a long short-term memory network (LSTM) can be used to solve the problems with RNN.

§ What Is an RNN?

A recurrent neural network is a type of neural network that is used to process data that is sequential in nature, e.g., stock price data, text sentences, or sales of items.

Sequential data is a type of data where the value of data at time step T depends upon the values of data at timesteps less than T. For instance, sound waves, text sentences, stock market prices, etc. In the stock market price prediction problem, the value of the opening price of a stock at a given data depends upon the opening stock price of the previous days.

The difference between the architecture of a recurrent neural network and a simple neural network is presented in the following figure:

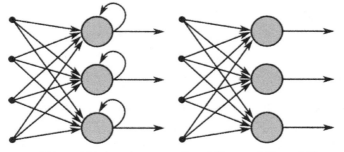

Recurrent Neural Network   Feed-Forward Neural Network

In a recurrent neural network, at each time step, the previous output of the neuron is also multiplied by the current input via a weight vector. You can see from the above figure that the output from a neuron is looped back into for the next time step. The following figure makes this concept further clear:

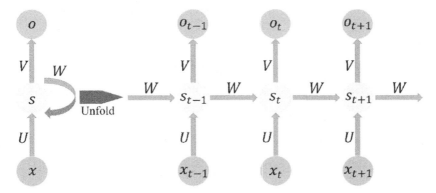

Here, we have a single neuron with one input and one output. On the right side, the process followed by a recurrent neural network is unfolded. You can see that at time step t, the input is multiplied by weight vector U, while the previous output at time t−1, i.e., St−1 is multiplied by the weight vector W, the sum of the input vector XU + SW becomes the output at time T. This is how a recurrent neural network captures the sequential information.

§ Problems with RNN

A problem with the recurrent neural network is that while it can capture a shorter sequence, it tends to forget longer sequences.

For instance, it is easier to predict the missing word in the following sentence because the Keyword "Birds" is present in the same sentence.

"Birds fly in the ____."

RNN can easily guess that the missing word is "Clouds" here.

However, RNN cannot remember longer sequences such as the one ...

"Mike grew up in France. He likes to eat cheese, he plays piano.. and
he speaks _____ fluently".

Here, the RNN can only guess that the missing word is "French" if it remembers the first sentence, i.e., "Mike grew up in France."

The recurrent neural networks consist of multiple recurrent layers, which results in a diminishing gradient problem. The diminishing gradient problem is that during the backpropagation of the recurrent layer, the gradient of the earlier layer becomes infinitesimally small, which virtually makes neural network initial layers stop from learning anything.

To solve this problem, a special type of recurrent neural network, i.e., Long Short-Term Memory (LSTM) has been developed.

§ What Is an LSTM?

LSTM is a type of RNN which is capable of remembering longer sequences, and hence, it is one of the most commonly used RNN for sequence tasks.

In LSTM, instead of a single unit in the recurrent cell, there are four interacting units, i.e., a forget gate, an input gate, an update gate, and an output gate. The overall architecture of an LSTM cell is shown in the following figure:

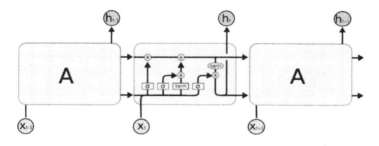

LSTM: Single Input - Single Output

Let's briefly discuss all the components of LSTM:

§ Cell State

The cell state in LSTM is responsible for remembering a long sequence. The following figure describes the cell state:

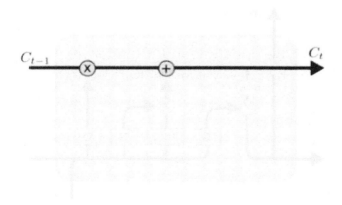

The cell state contains data from all the previous cells in the sequence. The LSTM is capable of adding or removing information to a cell state. In other words, LSTM tells the cell state which part of previous information to remember and which information to forget.

§ Forget Gate

The forget gate basically tells the cell state which information to retain from the information in the previous step and which information to forget. The working and calculation formula for the forget gate is as follows:

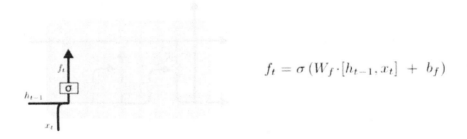

$$f_t = \sigma\left(W_f \cdot [h_{t-1}, x_t] + b_f\right)$$

§ Input Gate

The forget gate is used to decide which information to remember or forget. The input gate is responsible for updating or adding any new information in the cell state. The input gate has two parts: an input layer, which decides which part of the cell state is to be updated, and a tanh layer, which actually creates a vector of new values that are added or replaced in the cell state. The working of the input gate is explained in the following figure:

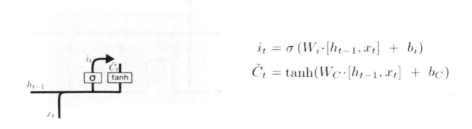

$$i_t = \sigma\left(W_i \cdot [h_{t-1}, x_t] + b_i\right)$$
$$\tilde{C}_t = \tanh(W_C \cdot [h_{t-1}, x_t] + b_C)$$

§ Update Gate

The forget gate tells us what to forget, and the input gate tells us what to add to the cell state. The next step is to actually perform these two operations. The update gate is basically used to perform these two operations. The functioning and the equations for the update gate are as follows:

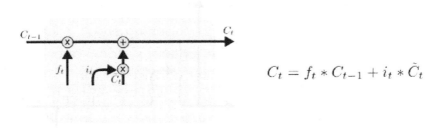

$$C_t = f_t * C_{t-1} + i_t * \tilde{C}_t$$

§ Output Gate

Finally, you have the output gate, which outputs the hidden state and the output, just like a common recurrent neural network. The additional output from an LSTM node is a cell state, which runs between all the nodes in a sequence. The equations and the functioning of the output gate are depicted by the following figure:

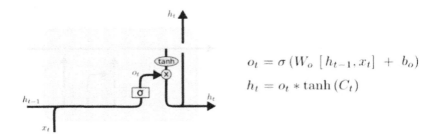

$$o_t = \sigma\left(W_o\left[h_{t-1}, x_t\right] + b_o\right)$$

$$h_t = o_t * \tanh\left(C_t\right)$$

In the following sections, you will see how to use LSTM for solving different types of Sequence problems.

9.3. Predicting Future Stock Prices via LSTM in Keras

Stock price prediction is one of the most common applications of many to one or many to many sequence problems.

In this section, we will predict the opening stock price of the Facebook company, using the opening stock price of the previous 60 days. The training set consists of the stock price data of Facebook from 1st January 2015 to 31st December 2019, i.e., five years. The dataset can be downloaded from this site:

https://finance.yahoo.com/quote/FB/history?p=FB.

The test data will consist of the opening stock prices of the Facebook company for the month of January 2020. The training file fb_train.csv and the test file fb_test.csv are also available in the *Datasets* folder in the GitHub repository. Let's begin with the coding now.

9.3.1. Training the Stock Prediction Model

In this section, we will train our stock prediction model on the training set.

Before you train the stock market prediction model, upload the TensorFlow version by executing the following command on Google collaborator (https://colab.research.google.com/).

Script 18:

```
pip install --upgrade tensorflow
```

If your files are placed on Google Drive, and you want to access them in Google Collaborator, to do so, you have to first mount the Google Drive inside your Google Collaborator environment via the following script:

Script 19:

```
1.  # mounting google drive
2.  from google.colab import drive
3.  drive.mount('/gdrive')
```

Next, to import the training dataset, execute the following script:

Script 20:

```
1.  # importing libraries
2.  import pandas as pd
3.  import numpy as np
4.
5.  #importing dataset
6.  fb_complete_data = pd.read_csv("/gdrive/My Drive/datasets/
    fb_train.csv")
```

Running the following script will print the first five rows of the dataset.

Script 21:

```
1.  #printing dataset header
2.  fb_complete_data.head()
```

Output:

	Date	Open	High	Low	Close	Adj Close	Volume
0	2015-01-02	78.580002	78.930000	77.699997	78.449997	78.449997	18177500
1	2015-01-05	77.980003	79.250000	76.860001	77.190002	77.190002	26452200
2	2015-01-06	77.230003	77.589996	75.360001	76.150002	76.150002	27399300
3	2015-01-07	76.760002	77.360001	75.820000	76.150002	76.150002	22045300
4	2015-01-08	76.739998	78.230003	76.080002	78.180000	78.180000	23961000

The output shows that our dataset consists of seven columns. However, in this section, we are only interested in the Open column. Therefore, we will select the Open column from the dataset. Run the following script to do so.

Script 22:

```
1.  #filtering open column
2.  fb_training_processed = fb_complete_data[['Open']].values
```

Next, we will scale our dataset.

Script 23:

```
1.  #scaling features
2.  from sklearn.preprocessing import MinMaxScaler
3.  scaler = MinMaxScaler(feature_range = (0, 1))
4.
5.  fb_training_scaled = scaler.fit_transform(fb_training_
    processed)
```

If you check the total length of the dataset, you will see it has 1257 records, as shown below:

Script 24:

```
1.  len(fb_training_scaled)
```

Output:

```
1257
```

Before we proceed further, we need to divide our data into features and labels. Our feature set will consist of 60 timesteps of 1 feature. The feature set basically consists of the opening stock price of the past 60 days, while the label set will consist of the opening stock price of 61st day. Based on the opening stock prices of the previous days, we will be predicted the opening stock price for the next day.

Script 25:

```
1.  #training features contain data of last 60 days
2.  #training labels contain data of 61st day
3.
4.  fb_training_features= []
5.  fb_training_labels = []
6.  for i in range(60, len(fb_training_scaled)):
7.      fb_training_features.append(fb_training_scaled[i-
    60:i, 0])
8.      fb_training_labels.append(fb_training_scaled[i, 0])
```

We need to convert our data into Numpy array before we can use as input with Keras. The following script does that:

Script 26:

```
1.  #converting training data to numpy arrays
2.  X_train = np.array(fb_training_features)
3.  y_train = np.array(fb_training_labels)
```

Let's print the shape of our dataset.

Script 27:

```
1.  print(X_train.shape)
2.  print(y_train.shape)
```

Output:

```
(1197, 60)
(1197,)
```

We need to reshape our input features into 3-dimensional format.

Script 28:

```
1.  converting data into 3D shape
2.  X_train = np.reshape(X_train, (X_train.shape[0], X_train.
    shape[1], 1))
```

The following script creates our LSTM model. We have 4 LSTM layers with 100 nodes each. Each LSTM layer is followed by a dropout layer to avoid overfitting. The final dense has one node since the output is a single value.

Script 29:

```
1.  #importing libraries
2.  import numpy as np
3.  import matplotlib.pyplot as plt
4.  from tensorflow.keras.layers import Input, Activation,
    Dense, Flatten, Dropout, Flatten, LSTM
5.  from tensorflow.keras.models import Model
```

Script 30:

```
1.  #defining the LSTM network
2.
3.  input_layer = Input(shape = (X_train.shape[1], 1))
4.  lstm1 = LSTM(100, activation='relu', return_
    sequences=True)(input_layer)
5.  do1 = Dropout(0.2)(lstm1)
6.  lstm2 = LSTM(100, activation='relu', return_
    sequences=True)(do1)
7.  do2 = Dropout(0.2)(lstm2)
8.  lstm3 = LSTM(100, activation='relu', return_
    sequences=True)(do2)
9.  do3 = Dropout(0.2)(lstm3)
10. lstm4 = LSTM(100, activation='relu')(do3)
11. do4 = Dropout(0.2)(lstm4)
12.
```

```
13. output_layer = Dense(1)(do4)
14. model = Model(input_layer, output_layer)
15. model.compile(optimizer='adam', loss='mse')
```

Next, we need to convert the output y into a column vector.

Script 31:

```
1.  print(X_train.shape)
2.  print(y_train.shape)
3.  y_train= y_train.reshape(-1,1)
4.  print(y_train.shape)
```

Output:

```
(1197, 60, 1)
(1197,)
(1197, 1)
```

The following script trains our stock price prediction model on the training set.

Script 32:

```
1.  #training the model
2.  model_history = model.fit(X_train, y_
    train, epochs=100, verbose=1, batch_size = 32)
```

You can see the results for the last five epochs in the output.

Output:

```
Epoch 96/100
38/38 [==============================] - 11s 299ms/step -
loss: 0.0018
Epoch 97/100
38/38 [==============================] - 11s 294ms/step -
loss: 0.0019
Epoch 98/100
38/38 [==============================] - 11s 299ms/step -
loss: 0.0018
```

```
Epoch 99/100
38/38 [==============================] - 12s 304ms/step -
loss: 0.0018
Epoch 100/100
38/38 [==============================] - 11s 299ms/step -
loss: 0.0021
```

Our model has been trained. Next, we will test our stock prediction model on the test data.

9.3.2. Testing the Stock Prediction Model

The test data should also be converted into the right shape to test our stock prediction model. We will do that later. Let's first import the data and then remove all the columns from the test data except the **Open** column.

Script 33:

```
1. #creating test set
2. fb_testing_complete_data = pd.read_csv("/gdrive/My Drive/
   datasets/fb_test.csv")
3. fb_testing_processed = fb_testing_complete_data[['Open']].
   values
```

Let's concatenate the training and test sets. We do this to predict the first value in the test set. The input will be the data from the past 60 days, which is basically the data from the last 60 days in the training set.

Script 34:

```
1. fb_all_data = pd.concat((fb_complete_data['Open'], fb_
   testing_complete_data['Open']), axis=0)
```

The following script creates our final input feature set.

Script 35:

```
1. test_inputs = fb_all_data [len(fb_all_data ) - len(fb_
   testing_complete_data) - 60:].values
2. print(test_inputs.shape)
```

You can see that the length of the input data is 80. Here, the first 60 records are the last 60 records from the training data, and the last 20 records are the 20 records from the test file.

Output:

```
(80,)
```

We need to scale our data and convert it into a column vector.

Script 36:

```
1. test_inputs = test_inputs.reshape(-1,1)
2. test_inputs = scaler.transform(test_inputs)
3. print(test_inputs.shape)
```

Output:

```
(80, 1)
```

As we did with the training data, we need to divide our input data into features and labels. Here is the script that does that.

Script 37:

```
1. fb_test_features = []
2. for i in range(60, 80):
3.     fb_test_features.append(test_inputs[i-60:i, 0])
```

Let's now print our feature set.

Script 38:

```
1. X_test = np.array(fb_test_features)
2. print(X_test.shape)
```

Output:

```
(20, 60)
```

Our feature set is currently 2-dimensional. But the LSTM algorithm in Keras accepts only data in 3-dimensional. The following script converts our input features into a 3-dimensional shape.

Script 39:

```
1. #converting test data into 3D shape
2. X_test = np.reshape(X_test, (X_test.shape[0], X_test.
   shape[1], 1))
3. print(X_test.shape)
```

Output:

```
(20, 60, 1)
```

Now is the time to make predictions on the test set. The following script does that:

Script 40:

```
1. #making predictions on test set
2. y_pred = model.predict(X_test)
```

Since we scaled our input feature, we need to apply the **inverse_transform()** method of the **scaler** object on the predicted output to get the original output values.

Script 41:

```
1. #converting scaled data back to original data
2. y_pred = scaler.inverse_transform(y_pred)
```

Finally, to compare the predicted output with the actual stock price values, you can plot the two values via the following script:

Script 42:

```
1. #plotting original and predicted stock values
2. plt.figure(figsize=(8,6))
3. plt.plot(fb_testing_processed, color='red', label='Actual
   Facenook Stock Price')
4. plt.plot(y_pred , color='green', label='Predicted Face
   Stock Price')
5. plt.title('Facebook Stock Prices')
6. plt.xlabel('Date')
7. plt.ylabel('Stock Price')
8. plt.legend()
9. plt.show()
```

Output:

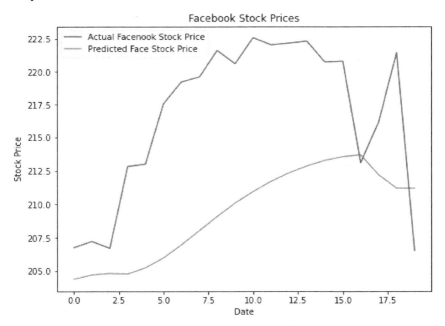

The output shows that our algorithm has been able to partially capture the trend of the future opening stock prices for Facebook data.

In the next section, you will see how to perform image classification using a convolutional neural network.

9.4. Convolutional Neural Network

A convolutional neural network is a type of neural network that is used to classify spatial data, for instance, images, sequences, etc. In an image, each pixel is somehow related to some other pictures. Looking at a single pixel, you cannot guess the image. Rather you have to look at the complete picture to guess the image. A CNN does exactly that. Using a kernel or feature detects, it detects features within an image. A combination of these images then forms the complete image, which can then be classified using a densely connected neural network. The steps involved in a Convolutional Neural Network have been explained in the next section.

9.4.1. Image Classification with CNN

In this section, you will see how to perform image classification using CNN. Before we go ahead and see the steps involved in the image classification using a convolutional neural network, we first need to know how computers see images.

§ How Do Computers See Images?

When humans see an image, they see lines, circles, squares, and different shapes. However, a computer sees an image differently. For a computer, an image is no more than a 2-D set of pixels arranged in a certain manner. For greyscale images, the pixel value can be between 0–255, while for color images, there are three channels: red, green, and blue. Each channel can have a pixel value between 0–255.

Look at the following image 9.1.

 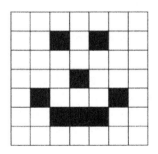 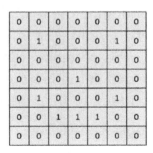

Image 9.1: How computers see images

Here, the box on the leftmost is what humans see. They see a smiling face. However, a computer sees it in the form of pixel values of 0s and 1s, as shown on the right-hand side. Here, 0 indicates a white pixel, whereas 1 indicates a black pixel. In the real-world, 1 indicates a white pixel, while 0 indicates a black pixel.

Now, we know how a computer sees images. The next step is to explain the steps involved in the image classification using a convolutional neural network.

The following are the steps involved in image classification with CNN:

1. The Convolution Operation
2. The ReLu Operation
3. The Pooling Operation
4. Flattening and Fully Connected Layer.

§ The Convolution Operation

The convolution operation is the first step involved in the image classification with a convolutional neural network.

In a convolution operation, you have an image and a feature detector. The values of the feature detector are initialized randomly. The feature detector is moved over the image from left to right. The values in the feature detector are multiplied by the corresponding values in the image, and then all the values in the feature detector are added. The resultant value is added to the feature map.

Look at the following image, for example:

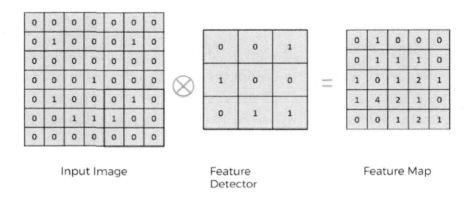

Input Image   Feature Detector   Feature Map

In the above image, we have an input image of 7 x 7. The feature detector is of the size 3 x 3. The feature detector is placed over the image at the top left of the input image, and then the pixel values in the feature detector are multiplied by the pixel values in the input image. The result is then added. The feature detector then moves to N step towards the right. Here, N refers to stride. A stride is basically the number of steps that a feature detector takes from left to right and then from top to bottom to find a new value for the feature map.

In reality, there are multiple feature detectors. As shown in the following image:

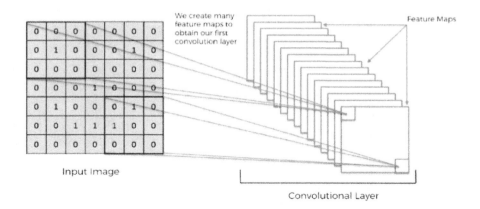

Input Image

Convolutional Layer

Each feature detector is responsible for detecting a particular feature in the image.

§ The ReLu Operation

In a ReLu operation, you simply apply the ReLu activation function on the feature map generated as a result of the convolution operation. A convolution operation gives us linear values. The ReLu operation is performed to introduce non-linearity in the image.

In the ReLu operation, all the negative values in a feature map are replaced by 0. All the positive values are left untouched.

Suppose we have the following feature map:

-4	2	1	-2
1	-1	8	0
3	-3	1	4
1	0	1	-2

When the ReLu function is applied on the feature map, the resultant feature map looks like this:

O	2	1	O
1	-O	8	O
3	O	1	4
1	O	1	O

§ The Pooling Operation

A pooling operation is performed in order to introduce spatial invariance in the feature map. Pooling operation is performed after convolution and ReLu operation.

Let's first understand what spatial invariance is. If you look at the following three images, you can easily identify that these images contain cheetahs.

Here, the second image is disoriented, and the third image is distorted. However, we are still able to identify that all the three images contain cheetahs based on certain features.

Pooling does exactly that. In pooling, we have a feature map and then a pooling filter, which can be of any size. Next, we move the pooling filter over the feature map and apply the pooling operation. There can be many pooling operations such as max pooling, min pooling, and average pooling. In max pooling, we choose the maximum value from the pooling filter. Pooling not only introduces spatial invariance but also reduces the size of an image.

Look at the following image. Here, in the 3rd and 4th rows and 1st and 2nd columns, we have four values 1, 0, 1, and 4. When we apply max pooling on these four pixels, the maximum value will be chosen, i.e., you can see 4 in the pooled feature map.

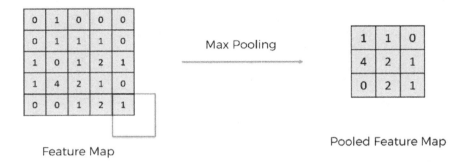

Feature Map   Pooled Feature Map

Max Pooling

§ Flattening and Fully Connected Layer

The pooled feature maps are flattened to form a one-dimensional vector to find more features from an image, as shown in the following figure:

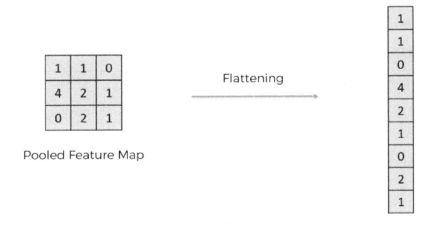

Pooled Feature Map

Flattening

The one-dimensional vector is then used as input to a densely or fully connected neural network layer that you saw in Chapter 4. This is shown in the following image:

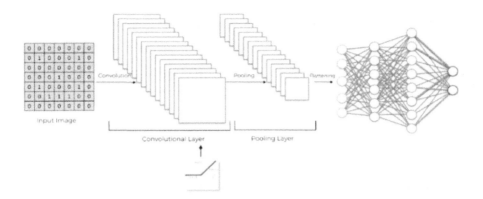

9.4.2. Implementing CNN with TensorFlow Keras

In this section, you will see how to implement CNN for image classification in TensorFlow Keras. We will create CNN that is able to classify an image of fashion items such as shirt, pants, trousers, sandals into one of the 10 predefined categories. So, let's begin without much ado.

Execute the following script to make sure that you are running the latest version of TensorFlow.

Script 43:

```
1.  pip install --upgrade tensorflow
2.
3.  import tensorflow as tf
4.  print(tf.__version__)
```

Output:

```
2.3.0
```

The following script imports the required libraries and classes.

Script 44:

```
1.  #importing required libraries
2.  import numpy as np
3.  import matplotlib.pyplot as plt
4.  from tensorflow.keras.layers import Input, Conv2D, Dense,
    Flatten, Dropout, MaxPool2D
5.  from tensorflow.keras.models import Model
```

The following script downloads the Fashion MNIST dataset that contains images of different fashion items along with their labels. The script divides the data into training images and training labels and test images and test labels.

Script 45:

```
1.  #importing mnist datase
2.  mnist_data = tf.keras.datasets.fashion_mnist
3.
4.  #dividing data into training and test sets
5.  (training_images, training_labels), (test_images, test_
    labels) = mnist_data .load_data()
```

The images in our dataset are greyscale images, where each pixel value lies between 0 and 255. The following script normalizes pixel values between 0 and 1.

Script 46:

```
1.  #scaling images
2.  training_images, test_images = training_images/255.0, test_
    images/255.0
```

Let's print the shape of our training data.

Script 47:

```
1.  print(training_images.shape)
```

Output:

```
(60000, 28, 28)
```

The above output shows that our training dataset contains 60,000 records (images). Each image is 28 pixels wide and 28 pixels high.

Let's print an image randomly from the test set:

Script 48:

```
1.  #plotting image number 9 from test set
2.  plt.figure()
3.  plt.imshow(test_images[9])
4.  plt.colorbar()
5.  plt.grid(False)
6.  plt.show()
```

Output:

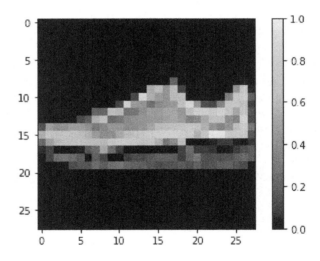

The output shows that the 9th image in our test set is the image of a sneaker.

The next step is to change the dimensions of our input images. CNN in Keras expects data to be in the format Width-Height-Channels. Our images contain width and height but no channels. Since the images are greyscale, we set the image channel to 1, as shown in the following script:

Script 49:

```
1.  #converting data into the right shape
2.  training_images = np.expand_dims(training_images, -1)
3.  test_images = np.expand_dims(test_images, -1)
4.  print(training_images.shape)
```

Output:

```
(60000, 28, 28, 1)
```

The next step is to find the number of output classes. This number will be used to define the number of neurons in the output layer.

Script 50:

```
1.  #printing number of output classes
2.  output_classes = len(set(training_labels))
3.  print("Number of output classes is: ", output_classes)
```

Output:

```
Number of output classes is:  10
```

As expected, the number of the output classes in our dataset is 10.

Let's print the shape of a single image in the training set.

Script 51:

```
1.  training_images[0].shape
```

Output:

```
(28, 28, 1)
```

The shape of a single image is (28, 28, 1). This shape will be used to train our convolutional neural network. The following script creates a model for our convolutional neural network.

Script 52:

```
1.  #Developing the CNN model
2.
3.  input_layer = Input(shape = training_images[0].shape )
4.  conv1 = Conv2D(32, (3,3), strides = 2, activation= 'relu')
    (input_layer)
5.  maxpool1 = MaxPool2D(2, 2)(conv1)
6.  conv2 = Conv2D(64, (3,3), strides = 2, activation= 'relu')
    (maxpool1)
7.  #conv3 = Conv2D(128, (3,3), strides = 2, activation=
    'relu')(conv2)
8.  flat1 = Flatten()(conv2)
9.  drop1 = Dropout(0.2)(flat1)
10. dense1 = Dense(512, activation = 'relu')(drop1)
11. drop2  = Dropout(0.2)(dense1)
12. output_layer = Dense(output_classes, activation=
    'softmax')(drop2)
13.
14. model = Model(input_layer, output_layer)
```

The model contains one input layer, two convolutional layers, one flattening layer, one hidden dense layer, in one output layer. The number of filters in the first convolutional layer is 32, while in the second convolutional layer, it is 64. The kernel size for both convolutional layers is 3 x 3, with a stride of 2. After the first convolutional layer, a max-pooling layer with a size 2 x 2 and stride 2 has also been defined.

It is important to mention that while defining the model layers, we used Keras Functional API. With Keras functional API, to connect the previous layer with the next layer, the name of the previous layer is passed inside the parenthesis at the end of the next layer.

The following line compiles the model.

Script 53:

```
1. #compiling the CNN model
2. model.compile(optimizer = 'adam', loss= 'sparse_
   categorical_crossentropy', metrics =['accuracy'])
```

Finally, execute the following script to print the model architecture.

Script 54:

```
1. from tensorflow.keras.utils import plot_model
2. plot_model(model, to_file='model_plot1.png', show_
   shapes=True, show_layer_names=True)
```

Output:

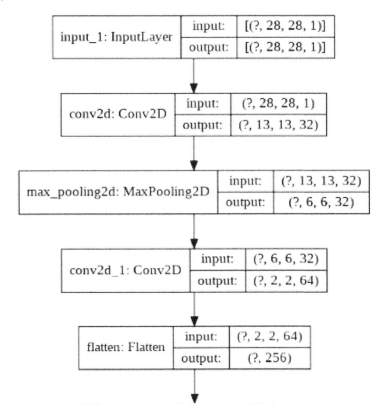

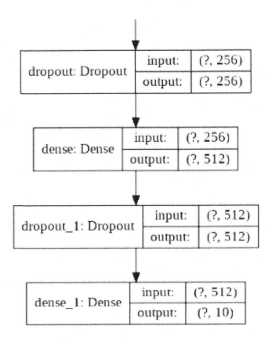

The following script trains the image classification model.

Script 55:

```
1.  #training the CNN model
2.  model_history = model.fit(training_images, training_
    labels, epochs=20, validation_data=(test_images, test_
    labels), verbose=1)
```

The results from the last five epochs are shown in the output.

Output:

```
Epoch 16/20
1875/1875 [==============================] - 5s 2ms/step - loss: 0.2318 - accuracy: 0.9107 - val_loss: 0.3217 - val_accuracy: 0.8843
Epoch 17/20
1875/1875 [==============================] - 4s 2ms/step - loss: 0.2269 - accuracy: 0.9129 - val_loss: 0.3268 - val_accuracy: 0.8870
Epoch 18/20
1875/1875 [==============================] - 4s 2ms/step - loss: 0.2224 - accuracy: 0.9147 - val_loss: 0.3379 - val_accuracy: 0.8814
Epoch 19/20
1875/1875 [==============================] - 4s 2ms/step - loss: 0.2164 - accuracy: 0.9174 - val_loss: 0.3279 - val_accuracy: 0.8846
Epoch 20/20
1875/1875 [==============================] - 4s 2ms/step - loss: 0.2112 - accuracy: 0.9192 - val_loss: 0.3277 - val_accuracy: 0.8882
```

Let's plot the training and test accuracies for our model.

Script 56:

```
1.  #plotting accuracy
2.  import matplotlib.pyplot as plt
3.
4.  plt.plot(model_history.
    history['accuracy'], label = 'accuracy')
5.  plt.plot(model_history.history['val_
    accuracy'], label = 'val_accuracy')
6.  plt.legend(['train','test'], loc='lower left')
```

The following output shows that training accuracy is higher, and test accuracy starts to flatten after 88 percent. We can say that our model is overfitting.

Output:

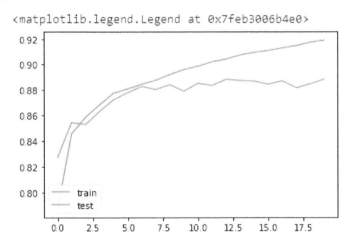

Let's make a prediction on one of the images in the test set. Let's predict the label for image 9. We know that image 9 contains a sneaker, as we saw earlier by plotting the image.

Script 57:

```
1.  #making predictions on a single image
2.  output = model.predict(test_images)
3.  prediction = np.argmax(output[9])
4.  print(prediction)
```

7

The output shows number 7. The output will always be a number since deep learning algorithms work only with numbers. The numbers correspond to the following labels:

0: T-shirt\top

1: Trousers

2: Pullover

3: Dress

4: Coat

5: Sandals

6: Shirt

7: Sneakers

8: Bag

9: Ankle boot

The above list shows that the number 7 corresponds to sneakers. Hence, the prediction by our CNN is correct.

In this chapter, you saw how to implement different types of deep neural networks, i.e., a densely connected neural network, a recurrent neural network, and a convolutional neural network with TensorFlow 2.0 and Keras library in Python.

Hands-on Time – Exercise

Now, it is your turn. Follow the instructions in **the exercises below** to check your understanding of the deep learning algorithms in TensorFlow 2.0. The answers to these exercises are provided after chapter 10 in this book.

Exercise 9.1

Question 1

What should be the input shape of the input image to the convolutional neural network?

   A. Width, Height

   B. Height, Width

   C. Channels, Width, Height

   D. Width, Height, Channels

Question 2

We say that a model is overfitting when:

   A. Results on test set are better than train set

   B. Results on both test and training sets are similar

   C. Results on the training set are better than the results on the test set

   D. None of the above

Question 3

The ReLu activation function is used to introduce:

   A. Linearity

   B. Non-linearity

   C. Quadraticity

   D. None of the above

Exercise 9.2

Using the CFAR 10 image dataset, perform image classification to recognize the image. Here is the dataset:

```
1.  cifar_dataset = tf.keras.datasets.cifar10
```

10

Dimensionality Reduction with PCA and LDA Using Sklearn

Dimensionality reduction refers to reducing the number of features in a dataset in such a way that the overall performance of the algorithms trained on the dataset is minimally affected. With dimensionality reduction, the training time of statistical algorithms can be significantly reduced, and data can be visualized more easily since it is not easy to visualize datasets in higher dimensions.

There are two main approaches used for dimensionality reduction: Principal Component Analysis (PCA) and Linear Discriminant Analysis (LDA). In this chapter, you will study both of them.

10.1. Principal Component Analysis

Principal component analysis is an unsupervised dimensionality reduction technique that doesn't depend on the labels of a dataset. Principal component analysis prioritizes features on the basis of their ability to cause maximum variance in the output. The idea behind PCA is to capture those features that contain maximum features about the dataset. The feature that causes the maximum variance in the output is called the first principal component, the feature that causes the second-highest variance is called the second principal component, and so on.

§ Why Use PCA?

The following are the advantages of PCA:

1. Correlated features can be detected and removed using PCA

2. Reduces overfitting because of reduction in the number of features

3. Model training can be expedited.

§ Disadvantages of PCA

There are two major disadvantages of PCA:

1. You need to standardize the data before you apply PCA

2. The independent variable becomes less integrable

3. Some amount of information is lost when you reduce features.

§ Implementing PCA with Python's Sklearn Library

In this section, you will see how to use PCA to select two of the most important features in the Iris dataset using the Sklearn library. The following script imports the required libraries:

Script 1:

```
1.  import pandas as pd
2.  import numpy as np
3.  import seaborn as sns
```

The following script imports the Iris dataset using the Seaborn library and prints the first five rows of the dataset.

Script 2:

```
1.  #importing the dataset
2.  iris_df = sns.load_dataset("iris")
3.
4.  #print dataset header
5.  iris_df.head()
```

Output:

	sepal_length	sepal_width	petal_length	petal_width	species
0	5.1	3.5	1.4	0.2	setosa
1	4.9	3.0	1.4	0.2	setosa
2	4.7	3.2	1.3	0.2	setosa
3	4.6	3.1	1.5	0.2	setosa
4	5.0	3.6	1.4	0.2	setosa

The above output shows that the dataset contains four features: sepal_length, sepal_width, petal_length, petal_width, and one output label, i.e., species. For PCA, we will only use the feature set.

The following script divides the data into the features and labels sets.

Script 3:

```
1.  #creating feature set
2.  X = iris_df.drop(['species'], axis=1)
3.
4.
5.  #creating label set
6.  y = iris_df["species"]
7.
8.  #converting labels to numbers
9.  from sklearn import preprocessing
10. le = preprocessing.LabelEncoder()
11. y = le.fit_transform(y)
```

Before we apply PCA on a dataset, we will divide it into the training and test sets, as shown in the following script.

Script 4:

```
1.  #dividing data into 80-20% traning and test sets
2.  from sklearn.model_selection import train_test_split
3.
4.  X_train, X_test, y_train, y_test = train_test_
    split(X, y,  test_size=0.20, random_state=0)
```

Finally, both the training and test sets should be scaled before PCA could be applied to them.

Script 5:

```
1.  #applying scaling on training and test data
2.  from sklearn.preprocessing import StandardScaler
3.  sc = StandardScaler()
4.  X_train = sc.fit_transform(X_train)
5.  X_test = sc.transform (X_test)
```

To apply PCA via Sklearn, all you have to do is import the PCA class from the Sklearn.decomposition module. Next, to apply PCA to the training set, pass the training set to the fit_tansform() method of the PCA class object. To apply PCA on the test set, pass the test set to the transform() method of the PCA class object. This is shown in the following script.

Script 6:

```
1.  #importing PCA class
2.  from sklearn.decomposition import PCA
3.
4.  #creating object of the PCA class
5.  pca = PCA()
6.
7.  #training PCA model on training data
8.  X_train = pca.fit_transform(X_train)
9.
10. #making predictions on test data
11. X_test = pca.transform(X_test)
```

Once you have applied PCA on a dataset, you can use the explained_variance_ratio_ feature to print variance caused by all the features in the dataset. This is shown in the following script:

Script 7:

```
1.  #printing variance ratios
2.  variance_ratios = pca.explained_variance_ratio_
3.  print(variance_ratios)
```

Output:

```
[0.72229951 0.2397406  0.03335483 0.00460506]
```

The output above shows that 72.22 percent of the variance in the dataset is caused by the first principal component, while 23.97 percent of the variance is caused by the second principal component.

Let's now select the two principal components that caused a collective variance of 96.19 percent (72.22% + 23.97% = 96.19%).

To select two principal components, all you have to do is pass 2 as a value to the n_components attribute of the PCA class. The following script selects two principal components from the Iris training and test sets.

Script 8:

```
1.  #use one principal component
2.  from sklearn.decomposition import PCA
3.
4.  pca = PCA(n_components=2)
5.  X_train = pca.fit_transform(X_train)
6.  X_test = pca.transform(X_test)
```

Let's train a classification model using logistic regression, which predicts the label of the iris plant using the two principal components or features, instead of the original four features.

Script 9:

```
1.  #making predictions using logistic regression
2.  from sklearn.linear_model import LogisticRegression
3.
4.  #training the logistic regression model
5.  lg = LogisticRegression()
6.  lg.fit(X_train, y_train)
7.
8.
9.  # Predicting the Test set results
10. y_pred = lg.predict(X_test)
11.
12. #evaluating results
13.
14. from sklearn.metrics import accuracy_score
15.
16. print(accuracy_score(y_test, y_pred))
```

Output:

```
0.8666666666666667
```

The output shows that even with two features, the accuracy for correctly predicting the label for the iris plant is 86.66.

Finally, with two features, you can easily visualize the dataset using the following script.

Script 10:

```
1.  from matplotlib import pyplot as plt
2.  %matplotlib inline
3.
4.  #print actual datapoints
5.
6.  plt.scatter(X_test[:,0], X_test[:,1], c= y_
    test, cmap='rainbow' )
```

Output:

<matplotlib.collections.PathCollection at 0x12ea1737610>

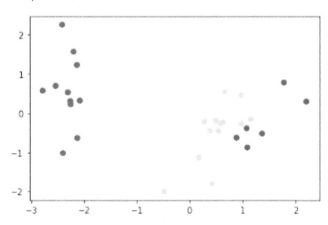

10.2. **Linear Discriminant Analysis**

Linear Discriminant Analysis (LDA) is a supervised dimen-sionality reduction technique, where a decision boundary is formed around data points belonging to each cluster of a class. The data points are projected to new dimensions in a way that the distance between the data points within a cluster is minimized, while the distance between the clusters is maximized. The new dimensions are ranked w.r.t. their ability to (i) minimize the distance between data points within a cluster, and (ii) maximize the distance between individual clusters.

§ Why Use LDA?

The following are the advantages of LDA:

1. Reduces overfitting because of reduction in the number of features

2. Model training can be expedited.

§ Disadvantages of LDA

There are three major disadvantages of LDA:

1. Not able to detect correlated features

2. Cannot be used with unsupervised or unlabeled data

3. Some amount of information is lost when you reduce features.

§ Implementing LDA with Sklearn Library

Let's see how you can implement LDA using the Sklearn library.

As always, the first step is to import the required libraries.

Script 11:

```
1.  import pandas as pd
2.  import numpy as np
3.  import seaborn as sns
```

You will be using the "banknote.csv" dataset from the *Datasets* folder in the GitHub repository. The following script imports the dataset and displays its first five rows.

Script 12:

```
1. #importing dataset
2. banknote_df = pd.read_csv(r"E:\Hands on Python for Data
   Science and Machine Learning\Datasets\banknote.csv")
3.
4. #displaying dataset header
5. banknote_df.head()
```

Output:

	variance	skewness	curtosis	entropy	class
0	3.62160	8.6661	-2.8073	-0.44699	0
1	4.54590	8.1674	-2.4586	-1.46210	0
2	3.86600	-2.6383	1.9242	0.10645	0
3	3.45660	9.5228	-4.0112	-3.59440	0
4	0.32924	-4.4552	4.5718	-0.98880	0

Let's divide the dataset into features and labels.

Script 13:

```
1. # dividing data into features and labels
2. X = banknote_df.drop(["class"], axis = 1)
3. y = banknote_df.filter(["class"], axis = 1)
```

Finally, the following script divides the data into training and test sets.

Script 14:

```
1. #dividing data into 80-20% training and test sets
2. from sklearn.model_selection import train_test_split
3.
4. X_train, X_test, y_train, y_test = train_test_
   split(X, y,  test_size=0.20, random_state=0)
```

Like PCA, you need to scale the data before you can apply LDA on it. The data scaling is performed in the following step.

Script 15:

```
1. #applying scaling on training and test data
2. from sklearn.preprocessing import StandardScaler
3. sc = StandardScaler()
4. X_train = sc.fit_transform(X_train)
5. X_test = sc.transform (X_test)
```

To apply LDA via Sklearn, all you have to do is import the LinearDiscriminantAnalysis class from the Sklearn. decomposition module. Next, to apply LDA to the training set, pass the training set to the fit_tansform() method of the LDA class object. To apply LDA on the test set, pass the test set to the transform() method of the LDA class object. This is shown in the following script.

Script 16:

```
1. #importing LDA class
2. from sklearn.discriminant_
   analysis import LinearDiscriminantAnalysis as LDA
3.
4.
5. #creating object of the LDA class
6. lda = LDA()
7.
8. #training PCA model on training data
9. X_train = lda.fit_transform(X_train, y_train)
10.
11. #making predictions on test data
12. X_test = lda.transform(X_test)
```

Like PCA, you can find variance ratios for LDA using the explained_variance_ratio attribute.

Script 17:

```
1. #printing variance ratios
2. variance_ratios = lda.explained_variance_ratio_
3. print(variance_ratios)
```

Output:

```
[1.]
```

The above output shows that even with one component, the maximum variance can be achieved.

Next, we select only a single component from our dataset using LDA. To do so, you have to pass 1 as the attribute value for the n_components attribute of the LDA class, as shown below.

Script 18:

```
1.  #creating object of the LDA class
2.  lda = LDA(n_components = 1)
3.
4.  #training PCA model on training data
5.  X_train = lda.fit_transform(X_train, y_train)
6.
7.  #making predictions on test data
8.  X_test = lda.transform(X_test)
```

Next, we will try to class whether or not a banknote is fake using a single feature. We will use the LogisticRegression algorithm for that. This is shown in the following script.

Script 19:

```
1.  #making predictions using logistic regression
2.  from sklearn.linear_model import LogisticRegression
3.
4.  #training the logistic regression model
5.  lg = LogisticRegression()
6.  lg.fit(X_train, y_train)
7.
8.
9.  # Predicting the Test set results
10. y_pred = lg.predict(X_test)
11.
```

```
12. #evaluating results
13.
14. from sklearn.metrics import accuracy_score
15.
16. print(accuracy_score(y_test, y_pred))
```

Output:

```
0.9890909090909091
```

The output shows that even with a single feature, we are able to correctly predict whether or not a banknote is fake with 98.90 percent accuracy.

Hands-on Time – Exercise

Now, it is your turn. Follow the instructions in **the exercises below** to check your understanding of the about dimensionality reduction using PCA and LDA. The answers to these exercises are provided after chapter 10 in this book.

Exercise 10.1

Question 1

Which of the following are the benefits of dimensionality reduction?

    A. Data Visualization

    B. Faster training time for statistical algorithms

    C. All of the above

    D. None of the above

Question 2

In PCA, dimensionality reduction depends upon the:

    A. Feature set only

    B. Label set only

    C. Both features and labels sets

    D. None of the above

Question 3

LDA is a _____ dimensionality reduction technique.

    A. Unsupervised

    B. Semi-Supervised

    C. Supervised

    D. Reinforcement

Exercise 10.2

Apply principal component analysis for dimensionality reduction on the customer_churn.csv dataset from the *Datasets* folder in the GitHub repository. Print the accuracy using the two principal components. Also, plot the results on the test set using the two principal components.

Exercises Solutions

Exercise 2.1

Question 1

Which iteration should be used when you want to repeatedly execute a code for a specific number of times?

  A. For Loop

  B. While Loop

  C. Both A and B

  D. None of the above

Answer: A

Question 2

What is the maximum number of values that a function can return in Python?

  A. Single Value

  B. Double Value

  C. More than two values

  D. None

Answer: C

Question 3

Which of the following membership operators are supported by Python?

    A. In

    B. Out

    C. Not In

    D. Both A and C

Answer: D

Exercise 2.2.

Print the table of integer 9 using a while loop:

```
1.  j=1
2.  while j< 11:
3.      print("9 x "+str(j)+ " = "+ str(9*j))
4.      j=j+1
```

Exercise 3.1

Question 1:

Which NumPy function is used for the element-wise multiplication of two matrices?

    A. np.dot(matrix1, matrix2)

    B. np.multiply(matrix1, matrix2)

    C. np.elementwise(matrix1, matrix2)

    D. None of the above

Answer: B

Question 2:

To generate an identity matrix of four rows and four columns, which of the following functions can be used?

    A. np.identity(4,4)

    B. np.id(4,4)

    C. np.eye(4,4)

    D. All of the above

Answer: C

Question 3:

How to create the array of numbers 4,7,10,13,16 with NumPy:

    A. np.arange(3, 16, 3)

    B. np.arange(4, 16, 3)

    C. np.arange(4, 15,3)

    D. None of the above

Answer: D

Exercise 3.2

Create a random NumPy array of five rows and four columns. Using array indexing and slicing, display the items from row three to end and column two to end.

Solution:

```
1.  uniform_random = np.random.rand(4, 5)
2.  print(uniform_random)
3.  print("Result")
4.  print(uniform_random[2:,3:])
```

Exercise 4.1

Question 1

In order to horizontally concatenate two Pandas dataframes, the value for the axis attribute should be set to:

    A. 0

    B. 1

    C. 2

    D. None of the above

Answer: B

Question 2

Which function is used to sort the Pandas dataframe by a column value?

    A. sort_dataframe()

    B. sort_rows()

    C. sort_values()

    D. sort_records()

Answer: C

Question 3

To filter columns from a Pandas dataframe, you have to pass a list of column names to one of the following method:

    A. filter()

    B. filter_columns()

    C. apply_filter ()

    D. None of the above()

Answer: A

Exercise 4.2

Use the apply function to subtract 10 from the Fare column of the Titanic dataset, without using the lambda expression.

Solution:

```
1.  def subt(x):
2.      return x - 10
3.
4.  updated_class = titanic_data.Fare.apply(subt)
5.  updated_class.head()
```

Exercise 5.1

Question 1

Which Pandas function is used to plot a horizontal bar plot:

    A. horz_bar()

    B. barh()

    C. bar_horizontal()

    D. horizontal_bar()

Answer: B

Question 2:

To create a legend, the value for which of the following parameters is needed to be specified?

    A. title

    B. label

    C. axis

    D. All of the above

Answer: B

Question 3:

How to show percentage values on a Matplotlib Pie Chart?

A. autopct = '%1.1f%%'

B. percentage = '%1.1f%%'

C. perc = '%1.1f%%'

D. None of the Above

Answer: A

Exercise 5.2

Plot two scatter plots on the same graph using the tips_ dataset. In the first scatter plot, display values from the total_bill column on the x-axis and from the tip column on the y-axis. The color of the first scatter plot should be green. In the second scatter plot, display values from the total_bill column on the x-axis and from the size column on the y-axis. The color of the second scatter plot should be blue, and the markers should be x.

Solution:

```
1.  sns.scatterplot(x="total_bill", y="tip", data=tips_data,
    color = 'g')
2.  sns.scatterplot(x="total_bill", y="size", data=tips_data,
    color = 'b', marker = 'x')
```

Output:

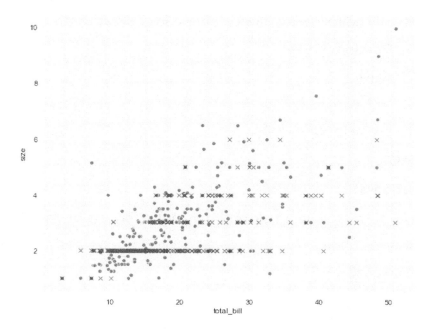

Exercise 6.1

Question 1

Among the following, which one is an example of a regression output?

    A. True

    B. Red

    C. 2.5

    D. None of the above

Answer: C

Question 2

Which of the following algorithm is a lazy algorithm?

    A. Random Forest

    B. KNN

    C. SVM

    D. Linear Regression

Answer: B

Question 3

Which of the following algorithm is not a regression metric?

    A. Accuracy

    B. Recall

    C. F1 Measure

    D. All of the above

Answer: D

Exercise 6.2

Using the *Diamonds* dataset from the Seaborn library, train a regression algorithm of your choice, which predicts the price of the diamond. Perform all the preprocessing steps.

Solution:

```
1. import pandas as pd
2. import numpy as np
3. import seaborn as sns
4.
5. diamonds_df = sns.load_dataset("diamonds")
6.
7. X = diamonds_df.drop(['price'], axis=1)
```

```
8.  y = diamonds_df["price"]
9.
10. numerical = X.drop(['cut', 'color', 'clarity'], axis = 1)
11.
12. categorical = X.filter(['cut', 'color', 'clarity'])
13.
14. cat_numerical = pd.get_dummies(categorical,drop_first=True)
15.
16. X = pd.concat([numerical, cat_numerical], axis = 1)
17.
18. from sklearn.model_selection import train_test_split
19.
20. X_train, X_test, y_train, y_test = train_test_
    split(X, y,  test_size=0.20, random_state=0)
21.
22. from sklearn.preprocessing import StandardScaler
23. sc = StandardScaler()
24. X_train = sc.fit_transform(X_train)
25. X_test = sc.transform (X_test)
26.
27. from sklearn import svm
28. svm_reg = svm.SVR()
29. regressor = svm_reg.fit(X_train, y_train)
30. y_pred = regressor.predict(X_test)
31.
32.
33.
34. from sklearn import metrics
35.
36. print('Mean Absolute Error:', metrics.mean_absolute_
    error(y_test, y_pred))
37. print('Mean Squared Error:', metrics.mean_squared_error(y_
    test, y_pred))
38. print('Root Mean Squared Error:', np.sqrt(metrics.mean_
    squared_error(y_test, y_pred)))
```

Exercise 7.1

Question 1

Among the following, which one is not an example of classification outputs?

    A. True

    B. Red

    C. Male

    D. None of the above

Answer: D

Question 2

Which of the following metrics is used for unbalanced classification datasets?

    A. Accuracy

    B. F1

    C. Precision

    D. Recall

Answer: C

Question 3

Which of the following function is used to convert categorical values to one-hot encoded numerical values?

    A. pd.get_onehot()

    B. pd.get_dummies()

    C. pd.get_numeric()

    D. All of the above

Answer: B

Exercise 7.2

Using the `iris` dataset from the Seaborn library, train a classification algorithm of your choice, which predicts the species of the iris plant. Perform all the preprocessing steps.

Solution:

```
1.  import pandas as pd
2.  import numpy as np
3.  import seaborn as sns
4.
5.  iris_df = sns.load_dataset("iris")
6.
7.  iris_df.head()
8.
9.  X = iris_df.drop(['species'], axis=1)
10. y = iris_df["species"]
11.
12.
13. from sklearn.model_selection import train_test_split
14.
15. X_train, X_test, y_train, y_test = train_test_
    split(X, y,  test_size=0.20, random_state=0)
16.
17. from sklearn.preprocessing import StandardScaler
18. sc = StandardScaler()
19. X_train = sc.fit_transform(X_train)
20. X_test = sc.transform (X_test)
21.
22. from sklearn.ensemble import RandomForestClassifier
23. rf_clf = RandomForestClassifier(random_state=42, n_
    estimators=500)
24.
25. classifier = rf_clf.fit(X_train, y_train)
26.
27. y_pred = classifier.predict(X_test)
28.
29.
```

```
30. from sklearn.metrics import classification_
    report, confusion_matrix, accuracy_score
31.
32. print(confusion_matrix(y_test,y_pred))
33. print(classification_report(y_test,y_pred))
34. print(accuracy_score(y_test, y_pred))
```

Exercise 8.1

Question 1

Which of the following is a supervised machine learning algorithm?

    A. K Means Clustering

    B. Hierarchical Clustering

    C. All of the above

    D. None of the above

Answer: D

Question 2

In KMeans clustering, what does the inertia tell us?

    A. the distance between data points within a cluster

    B. output labels for the data points

    C. the number of clusters

    D. None of the above

Answer: C

Question 3

In hierarchical clustering, in the case of vertical dendrograms, the number of clusters is equal to the number of _____ lines that the _____ line passes through?

    A. horizontal, vertical

    B. vertical, horizontal

    C. none of the above

    D. All of the above

Answer: B

Exercise 8.2

Apply KMeans clustering on the `banknote.csv` dataset available in the *Datasets* folder in the GitHub repository. Find the optimal number of clusters and then print the clustered dataset. The following script imports the dataset and prints the first five rows of the dataset.

```
1.  banknote_df = pd.read_csv(r"E:\
    Hands on Python for Data Science and Machine Learning\
    Datasets\banknote.csv")
2.  banknote_df.head()
3.
4.  ### Solution:
5.
6.  # dividing data into features and labels
7.  features = banknote_df.drop(["class"], axis = 1)
8.  labels = banknote_df.filter(["class"], axis = 1)
9.  features.head()
10.
11. # training KMeans on K values from 1 to 10
12. loss =[]
13. for i in range(1, 11):
```

```
14.    km = KMeans(n_clusters = i).fit(features)
15.    loss.append(km.inertia_)
16.
17. #printing loss against number of clusters
18.
19. import matplotlib.pyplot as plt
20. plt.plot(range(1, 11), loss)
21. plt.title('Finding Optimal Clusters via Elbow Method')
22. plt.xlabel('Number of Clusters')
23. plt.ylabel('loss')
24. plt.show()
25.
26. # training KMeans with 3 clusters
27. features = features.values
28. km_model = KMeans(n_clusters=2)
29. km_model.fit(features)
30.
31. #pring the data points with prediced labels
32. plt.scatter(features[:,0], features[:,1], c= km_model.
    labels_, cmap='rainbow' )
33.
34. #print the predicted centroids
35. plt.scatter(km_model.cluster_centers_[:, 0], km_model.
    cluster_centers_[:, 1], s=100, c='black')
```

Exercise 9.1

Question 1

What should be the input shape of the input image to the convolutional neural network?

    A. Width, Height

    B. Height, Width

    C. Channels, Width, Height

    D. Width, Height, Channels

Answer: (D)

Question 2:

We say that a model is overfitting when:

A. Results on the test set are better than the results on the training set

B. Results on both test and training sets are similar

C. Results on the training set are better than the results on the test set

D. None of the above

Answer (C)

Question 3

The ReLu activation function is used to introduce:

A. Linearity

B. Non-linearity

C. Quadraticity

D. None of the above

Answer: (B)

Exercise 9.2

Using the CFAR 10 image dataset, perform image classification to recognize the image. Here is the dataset:

```
2.  cifar_dataset = tf.keras.datasets.cifar10
```

Solution:

```
1.  #importing required libraries
2.  import numpy as np
3.  import matplotlib.pyplot as plt
4.  from tensorflow.keras.layers import Input, Conv2D, Dense,
    Flatten, Dropout, MaxPool2D
```

```
5. from tensorflow.keras.models import Model
6.
7.
8. (training_images, training_labels), (test_images, test_
   labels) = cifar_dataset.load_data()
9.
10. training_images, test_images = training_images/255.0,
    test_images/255.0
11.
12. training_labels, test_labels = training_labels.flatten(),
    test_labels.flatten()
13. print(training_labels.shape)
14. print(training_images.shape)
15. output_classes = len(set(training_labels))
16. print("Number of output classes is: ", output_classes)
17. input_layer = Input(shape = training_images[0].shape )
18. conv1 = Conv2D(32, (3,3), strides = 2, activation= 'relu')
    (input_layer)
19. maxpool1 = MaxPool2D(2, 2)(conv1)
20. conv2 = Conv2D(64, (3,3), strides = 2, activation= 'relu')
    (maxpool1)
21. #conv3 = Conv2D(128, (3,3), strides = 2, activation=
    'relu')(conv2)
22. flat1 = Flatten()(conv2)
23. drop1 = Dropout(0.2)(flat1)
24. dense1 = Dense(512, activation = 'relu')(drop1)
25. drop2  = Dropout(0.2)(dense1)
26. output_layer = Dense(output_classes, activation=
    'softmax')(drop2)
27.
28. model = Model(input_layer, output_layer)
29. model.compile(optimizer = 'adam', loss= 'sparse_
    categorical_crossentropy', metrics =['accuracy'])
30. model_history = model.fit(training_images, training_labels,
    epochs=20, validation_data=(test_images, test_labels),
    verbose=1)
```

Exercise 10.1

Question 1

Which of the following are the benefits of dimensionality reduction?

    A. Data Visualization

    B. Faster training time for statistical algorithms

    C. All of the above

    D. None of the above

Answer: C

Question 2

In PCA, dimensionality reduction depends upon the:

    A. Feature set only

    B. Label set only

    C. Both features and labels sets

    D. None of the above

Answer: A

Question 3

LDA is a _____ ? dimensionality reduction technique

    A. Unsupervised

    B. Semi-Supervised

    C. Supervised

    D. Reinforcement

Answer: C

Exercise 10.2

Apply principal component analysis for dimensionality reduction on the customer_churn.csv dataset from the *Datasets* folder in the GitHub repository. Print the accuracy using the two principal components. Also, plot the results on the test set using the two principal components.

Solution:

```
1.  import pandas as pd
2.  import numpy as np
3.
4.  churn_df = pd.read_csv("E:\Hands on Python for Data Science
    and Machine Learning\Datasets\customer_churn.csv")
5.  churn_df.head()
6.
7.  churn_df = churn_df.drop(['RowNumber', 'CustomerId',
    'Surname'], axis=1)
8.
9.  X = churn_df.drop(['Exited'], axis=1)
10. y = churn_df['Exited']
11.
12. numerical = X.drop(['Geography', 'Gender'], axis = 1)
13. categorical = X.filter(['Geography', 'Gender'])
14. cat_numerical = pd.get_dummies(categorical,drop_first=True)
15. X = pd.concat([numerical, cat_numerical], axis = 1)
16. X.head()
17.
18. from sklearn.model_selection import train_test_split
19.
20. X_train, X_test, y_train, y_test = train_test_split(X, y,
    test_size=0.20, random_state=0)
21.
22. #applying scaling on training and test data
23. from sklearn.preprocessing import StandardScaler
24. sc = StandardScaler()
25. X_train = sc.fit_transform(X_train)
26. X_test = sc.transform (X_test)
```

```
27.
28. #importing PCA class
29. from sklearn.decomposition import PCA
30.
31. #creating object of the PCA class
32. pca = PCA()
33.
34. #training PCA model on training data
35. X_train = pca.fit_transform(X_train)
36.
37. #making predictions on test data
38. X_test = pca.transform(X_test)
39.
40. #printing variance ratios
41. variance_ratios = pca.explained_variance_ratio_
42. print(variance_ratios)
43.
44. #use one principal component
45. from sklearn.decomposition import PCA
46.
47. pca = PCA(n_components=2)
48. X_train = pca.fit_transform(X_train)
49. X_test = pca.transform(X_test)
50.
51. #making predictions using logistic regression
52. from sklearn.linear_model import LogisticRegression
53.
54. #training the logistic regression model
55. lg = LogisticRegression()
56. lg.fit(X_train, y_train)
57.
58.
59. # Predicting the Test set results
60. y_pred = lg.predict(X_test)
61.
62. #evaluating results
63.
64. from sklearn.metrics import accuracy_score
65.
```

```
66. print(accuracy_score(y_test, y_pred))
67.
68. from matplotlib import pyplot as plt
69. %matplotlib inline
70.
71. #print actual datapoints
72.
73. plt.scatter(X_test[:,0], X_test[:,1], c= y_
    test, cmap='rainbow' )
```

Made in the USA
Monee, IL
18 September 2021

78330495R00167